THE GREEN CRAFTER

The GREEN Crafter

52
Eco-Friendly Projects
for Every Week of the Year

Richela Fabian Morgan

CITADEL PRESS
Kensington Publishing Corp.
www.kensingtonbooks.com

CITADEL PRESS BOOKS are published by

Kensington Publishing Corp.
850 Third Avenue
New York, NY 10022

Copyright © 2009 Richela Fabian Morgan

All Kensington titles, imprints, and distributed lines are available at special quantity discounts for bulk purchases for sales promotions, premiums, fund-raising, educational, or institutional use. Special book excerpts or customized printings can also be created to fit specific needs. For details, write or phone the office of the Kensington special sales manager: Kensington Publishing Corp., 850 Third Avenue, New York, NY 10022, attn: Special Sales Department; phone 1-800-221-2647.

CITADEL PRESS and the Citadel logo are Reg. U.S. Pat. & TM Off.

First printing: June 2009

10 9 8 7 6 5 4 3 2 1

Printed in the United States of America

Library of Congress Control Number: 2008942174

ISBN-13: 978-0-8065-3120-5
ISBN-10: 0-8065-3120-7

To Norma Masana Fabian, my mother and inspiration for all crafty things.
And to Masana Mae Morgan, my beautiful daughter and pocket muse.

Contents

September

October

November

December

Introduction

The Fourth "R"

OKAY, WE GET IT BY NOW: the mantra of the twenty-first century is to GO GREEN. We reduce, we reuse, and we recycle. These three R's have infused our everyday existence, from the moment we open our eyes in the morning until the last random thought leaves our head at night. We sort our trash with a militaristic eye, dispatching harsh reprimands to anyone (son, friend, total stranger) when a plastic container finds its way into the paper bin. We've switched all light fixtures in the house to those compact fluorescent lightbulbs, regardless of how their bluish tint exaggerates every wrinkle and dark circle on our face. And we purchase as much organic produce as our shrinking wallets will allow, making meals more like lite beer (more taste but less filling).

We've added such words as *sustainability* and *practicality* to our daily vocabulary. We constantly ask ourselves "Do I really need . . . ?" when admiring a pair of shoes in a store window or contemplating raising the home thermostat. We fear the size of our carbon footprint may be too great to bear, so we cut back on those small luxuries that make life a little easier. And the GO GREEN mantra has spawned fanatics that zealously rant and rave every time they come across a poor soul who has not already drunk the proverbial Kool-Aid, thus proving that antagonism and altruism are not mutually exclusive. To make matters worse, some of these fanatics are celebrities who use their media clout to rain gloom and doom on our sunny lives.

So the mantra has essentially become a threat: reduce, reuse, and recycle OR ELSE—dum, dum, dum—you die!

Yes, we must GO GREEN, embrace the three R's as we do our own family members—even the ones we don't like (and you know that you have at least one that really rubs you the wrong way). But it is time to amend the mantra to include a fourth and equally important R: reinvention. It is time to acknowledge that saving the planet can also be fun. The reinvention part of the GO GREEN mantra is more uplifting from the other R's because it frees you from direct social or environmental responsibility. Yes, you are saving some trash from a landfill, but the main purpose of reinvention is to satisfy a creative urge.

How do we reinvent? We give an object a new life by finding another purpose. Kids do it everyday when they take a cardboard box and pretend it's a rocket ship or a clubhouse. Why can't conscientious and sensible adults do the same? However, the transformation from garbage to art object is not so immediate. If you have some experience with any type of craft, reinventing an object bound for the trash may not be difficult. You are already familiar with the type of materials you need, so finding substitutes in everyday junk may not be such a stretch. But new crafters may need to be a bit more patient.

There are several questions you must ask of a heap of trash before finding the form. Will that magazine yield any decent folding paper, which you can then use to make origami or tea bag folded flowers (for a card you are going to make for your mother in three weeks)? Can those plastic container lids make wheels that will be a part of a toy car (also made from a corrugated box you've been saving until you could find something to use for the wheels)?

In this book, I've listed materials at the beginning of each chapter so you can get a sense of what you need to save and avoid the swells of bags with unusable garbage. The process of saving materials can get messy, so you should always have some idea of what you want to make ahead of time. The more you do it, the better your sense develops of what can be saved. For example, buttons, half-gallon cartons, paper clips, and cereal boxes are staple materials in all my crafts, so I save them all the time. I have neat and appropriately sized containers for these materials. Egg cartons and paper towel rolls are not something I use frequently. But I do try to save them prior to the winter holidays when my kids and I have more time to craft together.

This book contains projects to inspire all you budding crafters of reinvention, whether you are a motivated neophyte, an insanely particular and experienced crafter, or somewhere in between. They easily adapt to whatever recycling material you may have around the home, so you might feel like McGyver, our beloved mullet-wearing eighties television hero who could make a useful item out of, let's say, a piece of chewing gum, some paper clips, and a drinking straw. No drinking straw? That's fine. Use a chopstick. No chopstick? Well, then, a pencil might work . . .

You see where I'm going with this?

Reduce. Reuse. Recycle. Reinvent!

MATERIALS FROM YOUR HOME

Before you toss something in the trash can, give it another look. Maybe that milk carton can be a doll's bed, or the latest issue of *Vogue* could supply ample sheets of origami paper. Try to write down your ideas and break out the items that may be used. Try to be realistic about the project and the materials. For instance, making a bracelet out of broken plates may be a hard task to accomplish. (Of course, this is a quite ridiculous example . . .)

Finding Suitable Materials

The following are some of the items you might want to save for a craft project:

Paper items

magazine

newspaper

junk mail

business card

flier

used printer paper

gift wrap

tissue paper
   (NOT tissue!)

deck of cards
   (if incomplete)

greeting card

corrugated box

cereal or cookie box

juice or milk carton

egg carton

toilet or paper towel roll

inserts for linen or
   T-shirt package

brown paper bag

Plastic items

lidded dairy container
   (e.g., from sour cream
   or whipped butter)

liquid container

button

bead

vitamin bottle

fruit net bag

detergent container

bread bag

plastic shopping bag
   (from a retail or
   grocery store)

dried-up pen

Metal, glass, or wood items

chopstick

jar

coffee can

bottle cap

pencil

dried-up pen

paper clip

wine cork

salad dressing bottle

wire from spiral
   notebook

Cloth items

100% cotton pajamas or
   T-shirt

sock

children's tights

towel

canvas bag

anything denim

ribbon and cord

Toys

jigsaw pieces (if puzzle is
   incomplete)

ripped or otherwise
   damaged picture book

board game and pieces

Ping-Pong ball

Tips for Setting Up Your Work Space

Your work space should consist of a clear tabletop, a cutting mat, and ample waste paper sheets. Be sure to have your tools close enough to reach but at a distance that will not interfere with your work. Be mindful where you leave small sharp tools and never rush through a project. Accidents can and will happen!

Lest your tabletop becomes an unmanageable mess of used CDs and cereal boxes, here are a few tips to keep things neat:

1. Designate a specific area to store your materials. Use corrugated boxes to store the larger items and coffee cans or jars to organize the smaller ones.

2. Keep sharp or breakable objects out of reach of small children by placing the items in a covered bin, toolbox, or tackle box.

3. If the items are large, you may want to put them away in a closet or a high shelf.

4. If the item previously contained food, be sure to clean it very well before storing it. Wash it out and allow enough time for the container to dry.

5. Cardboard boxes should be flattened; stickers or tape should be removed. Try to not make new folds or creases.

6. If you are collecting small items, try to store them in a container with a lid.

7. Try to keep extra waste sheets on hand, which can be made from brown paper bags that have been taken apart at the seams. Also see page xv.

8. Try to keep a spray bottle containing water and a dry cotton cloth for quick cleanups.

9. Try to write down your ideas so you don't wind up saving things and not using them.

10. If you haven't used something for a while and it's taking up space, throw it out! Chances are, you will come across another one just like it sometime down the road.

Tools and How to Use Them

Here's a quick primer on how to use some common and not-so-common tools of the trade. Don't worry if you don't have some of them. In most cases, household items may be used in their place. But for the sake of understanding the directions in this book, please review this list so you don't wind up scratching your head at every turn or cursing the author (that would be me) for creating such an impossible project.

THE NOT-SO-FAMILIAR

Awl

What it is: primarily a woodworking tool, it has a wooden handle and a short metal rod with a pointed tip.

What it should be used for: poking holes.

What you can substitute if you don't have/want one: an embroidery needle, or use a regular needle to make a small hole and then a dried-up pen to enlarge it.

Bone folder

What it is: it resembles a letter opener, somewhat pointed at one end, and usually made of polished bone or hard plastic.

What it should be used for: to fold, score, or burnish paper or cardboard.

What you can substitute if you don't have/want one: if you're scoring something, use a dried-up pen; if you're folding something, use the side of a pencil.

Brayer

What it is: a small hand roller typically made of acrylic or rubber. Initially a printer's tool to spread ink, it is primarily used in scrapbooking.

What it should be used for: to smooth surfaces, flatten paper, or apply inks. In this book, we use a brayer to remove air pockets and to smooth surfaces.

What you can substitute if you don't have/want one: a bone folder or the flat side of a ruler.

Craft knife

What it is: a short cutting blade attached to a penlike handle.

What it should be used for: cutting paper or other materials that cannot be cut by scissors or paper cutter; cutting out fine details.

What you can substitute if you don't have/want one: box cutter.

Hand weights

What it is: well, just what you imagine this would be: an actual hand weight of the gym variety, 5 to 10 pounds. Or anything that is heavy enough to hold something down: a textbook, a paperweight, or a box full of nails.

What it should be used for: to hold objects in place when gluing them together, or to ensure boards or paper does not ripple, waffle, or curl when the adhesive is drying

What you can substitute if you don't have/want one: just find a heavy household object: a cast-iron pan, any sealable container you can fill with water or sand, or a large rock

Microspatula

What it is: a long metal instrument with flat ends

What it should be used for: pushing in tight corners or working glue into small spaces

What you can substitute if you don't have/want one: a bamboo stick, pencil

Pin tool

What it is: a sculptor's tool, it is a long metal pin with a wooden handle

What it should be used for: poking small holes

What you can substitute if you don't have/want one: a thick sewing needle

PVA

What it is: polyvinyl acetate, a nonacidic adhesive; a.k.a. "white glue"

What it should be used for: most bookmakers use PVA mixed with methyl cellulose (nontoxic solvent) to adhere a substrate (e.g., bookcloth, paper) to a board or the spine of a book block

What you can substitute if you don't have/want one: regular old Elmer's Glue-All

Round-nose pliers

What it is: a jewelry crafting tool; the two prongs of the pliers are rounded

What it should be used for: to bend metal or wire in a circular manner.

What you can substitute if you don't have/want one: regular pliers (try adding artist's tape for a softer grip)

Tweezers

What it is: a jewelry crafting tool as well as a makeup accessory tool

What it should be used for: picking up small objects, such as rhinestones or beads

What you can substitute if you don't have/want one: chopsticks or your fingernails

USEFUL TIPS ABOUT THE FAMILIAR

Self-healing cutting mat

Try to clean the mat after every use, with a wet cloth. Sometimes excess glue will find its way onto the surface and spoil your next project. Do not leave your mat in the sun or on top of a radiator or else it will warp.

Glue

White paste, such as Elmer's Glue-All is thinner than tacky glue.

Tacky glue versus a glue stick: although a glue stick is much easier (and cleaner) to work with, it only works with paper. Nonpaper objects such as buttons or ribbon will not stick to your intended surface unless you use tacky glue.

Fabric glue doesn't harden completely, so using it as a substitute for other types of glue may not be the best idea.

Carpenter's glue is great for adhering porous objects together. If the surface is slick or varnished in any way, the glue will lift right off after it dries. It does not dry clear, whereas the other glues do.

Paint

Benjamin Moore makes sample preview containers of such a wide range of colors. If you don't live near a craft or art supply shop, it's a bit cheaper and more accessible to purchase acrylic paints—a quick trip to your local hardware store will suffice. Acrylic is water-based latex paint, so if you are making a costume for your child, make sure he or she is not allergic to it.

Paper cutter

The rotary type is preferred over the guillotine one. It's safer to have around a house full of children (and clumsy adults). It also cuts more accurately.

Paintbrush

Besides the obvious use of a paintbrush, you can use it to gently get rid of any air bubbles when adhering paper or cloth to a surface. (Sometimes, using a bone folder to do this will damage the material.) Keeping one or two dry brushes around might come in handy.

Pencil

The best pencils to use are ones that will draw lightly and erase well, like a B or HB. And get a good eraser, such as Magic Rub.

Chain-nose pliers

Putting some artist's tape on the ends can prevent your pliers' leaving scratches or tears on the material you are working with.

Ruler

Always get a metal ruler with a cork backing. When you are cutting material with a craft knife, a metal ruler is needed to cut against to ensure a straight edge. The cork backing will hold the ruler in place. A metal ruler can also serve as a scoring tool. Having two rulers instead of just one is helpful, especially if you have two different sizes (2 foot and 1 foot).

Waste sheets

You can make waste sheets from just about anything: newspaper, brown paper bags from the grocery store, paper that you've used both sides of. Try to keep a healthy supply of waste sheets, or simply keep your paper recycle bin close by.

Types of tape

Artist's: white tape, thick and almost clothlike. Makes great impromptu hinges.

Masking: when you're making papier-mâché, masking tape is great for holding your paper items together and is easy to paint over.

Packing: who says it's only for putting packages together? Clear packing tape can be used as a transparent paper laminate, such as for kids' place mats.

Duct: because it comes in so many different colors, this tape can replace paper or cloth when you're making just about anything.

Double-sided: can sometimes be used in lieu of a glue stick. It's more forgiving than glue

Electrical: it comes in a wide variety of colors and can be more decorative than useful.

Painter's: in blue or purple, it's great to use when temporarily marking something on your project as well as to prevent paint from getting on areas of your project that should remain paint-free.

Cellophane: the old standard. Need I say anything else?

BEFORE YOU START

There are just a few things you should know before you jump ahead to the crafts.

HOW TO MAKE "THE MIX"

In this book, many card-, book-, or box-related projects call for "the mix." What is "the mix," you might ask. It is a combination of PVA and methyl cellulose. Bookmakers around the world will nod their heads and say, "Ah, the mix . . ."

PVA is polyvinyl acetate, or white glue. It is pH balanced and dries quickly. You can purchase it in craft and art supply stores. Methyl cellulose is an organic gel substance that is found in powder form in most craft and art supply stores. Thoroughly mix 1 tablespoon of the powder with 2 cups of cold water and let it stand for 15 minutes.

"The mix" is a combination of 70 percent PVA and 30 percent methyl cellulose. Adding the methyl cellulose to PVA makes it dry slower and be a bit more flexible when dry. It is used primarily in book and box making because it also does not warp the material (usually paper or boards) as it dries. It should be thinly applied with a 1-inch brush to any surface you are gluing. You can make large amounts of "the mix" and store it in sealable containers at room temperature.

MAKING PAPIER-MÂCHÉ PASTE

    1 cup all-purpose flour
    1 cup hot water
    1 cup cold water

Mix thoroughly with a whisk to get out the lumps.

For the serving bowls on page 94, you may want to thin out the paste by adding another cup of cold water.

HOW TO DO A BLANKET STITCH

1. Working from left to right, begin a new stitch by pushing the needle along the edge of fabric, through the back and then pulling the needle toward you.

2. As you pull at the slack, be sure to push the needle through the shrinking loop.

3. Pull the needle and thread until no slack remains.

4. Repeat steps 1 through 3.

THE GREEN CRAFTER

January

Projects This Month

Your Average Little Notepad
Rolled Bead Bracelet
"Sock" Monkey
Universal Little Wallet
Cardboard House

THE FIRST MONTH OF EVERY YEAR presents us with a clean slate, a fresh start. Each of us vainly puts pen to paper and scribbles down a list of things to achieve: a slimmer physique, a less-cluttered closet, better eating habits, and maybe, just maybe, a few more dollars in the bank. But what about saving the environment? Too lofty a goal, perhaps? And why not? Just because you cannot easily quantify it by looking in the mirror or at your bank statements? But what if you could save the environment while making things that are useful, attractive, and just plain cool? Would you do it then?

You won't win a Nobel Prize for doing your part to save the planet, but then again, you're not supposed to do it for the glory. It's all about turning inward and rewarding yourself. So give yourself a pat on the back because the new you for the New Year is an eco-conscious you, a healthier person in every facet of life.

Sound good? Are you with me? Let's begin.

Materials you will need this month

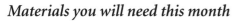

2 cardboard boxes (cookie, cereal, or dishwasher detergent box)
20 pieces scrap paper, at least 5 × 7 inches each
2 magazine sheets
1 button/round/at least ¾ inch in diameter
1 pair tights (2 pairs would be nice but not necessary) children's
Leftover yarn or embroidery floss, about 3 yards or 9 feet of one color
Leftover yarn or embroidery floss in red, black, and blue
An old pillow (preferably with synthetic stuffing)
1 gift bag (paper, not plastic)
1 brown paper grocery bag
1 Velcro tab

2 corrugated boxes, medium or large size

Lots of string

Barbecue skewers

1 small coin (obsolete ones from any of the Western European countries that now use the euro, or from an arcade)

January holidays, typical and not-so

New Year's Day (1st)

Festival of Sleep Day (3rd)

Feast of the Epiphany (6th)

Man Watcher's Day (8th)

Feast of Fabulous Wild Men (12th)

National Dress Up Your Pet Day (14th)

Hat Day (15th)

Winnie the Pooh Day (18th)

National Popcorn Day (19th)

National Hugging Day (21st)

Martin Luther King, Jr. Day (3rd Monday)

National Pie Day (23rd)

Opposite Day (25th)

National Kazoo Day (28th)

Monthlong celebrations

National Blood Donor Month

National Braille Literacy Month

National Careers in Cosmetology Month

National Eye Health Care Month

National Fiber Focus Month

National Hobby Month

National Soup Month

Hot Tea Month

Oatmeal Month

Prune Breakfast Month

National Thank-You Month

January birthdays of famous people

Betsy Ross (1st)

J. D. Salinger (1st)

Millard Fillmore (7th)

Elvis Presley (8th)

Alexander Hamilton (11th)

Dr. Martin Luther King, Jr. (15th)

Ethel Merman (16th)

Benjamin Franklin (17th)

Muhammad Ali (17th)

John Hancock (23rd)

Neil Diamond (24th)

Paul Newman (26th)

Franklin D. Roosevelt (30th)

1. Your Average Little Notepad

BEFORE WRITING DOWN those New Year's resolutions, you will need a notepad. But instead of going out and buying one, why not make one?

It's easy, it's quick, and it's really, really addictive. Once you finish making this basic notepad, a sense of empowerment will take over. You'll think, "Hey that was really easy!" Or maybe, "Boy, can I sure make twenty more of those!" And the next thing you know, you're adding a little twist to the stitch binding here or a cover embellishment there. You've become a notepad-making monster, and, unfortunately, there are no twelve step programs for you.

The good news is that notepads are just the tip of the iceberg known as bookmaking. There are dozens of other types of books to make. Check out *How to Make Books* by Esther K. Smith or *500 Handmade Books: Inspiring Interpretations of a Timeless Form* by Lark.

Materials

1 small cardboard box, at least 5 × 6 × 3 inches
20 pieces scrap paper, each piece no smaller than 5 × 7 inches
1 piece colored string, approximately 4 feet long

Tools

Craft knife	Awl
Paper cutter	Thick needle
Metal ruler	Beeswax
Bone folder	Scissors
Pencil	

Tips

- The size of your box may differ slightly from the one in the instructions. Read through the directions first before beginning the project, just in case you need to make any adjustments to your measurements.
- Remember that the size of the outer case always dictates the size of the paper, and never the other way around.

Outer case

1. Take the **box** apart at the glued seams. Lay the box flat on the cutting mat. Using the metal ruler and craft knife, cut off the top, bottom, left outer side, and right outer sides of the box. You should have three panels remaining.

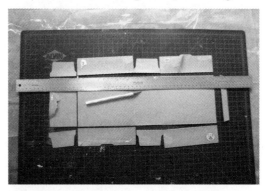

2. Using the ruler and pencil, mark the vertical center at the top and bottom of the middle panel. Draw a line from the top to the bottom. Place your metal ruler along the line and score the box with the bone folder.

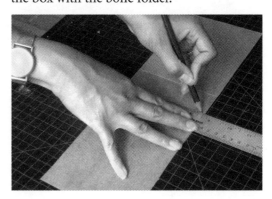

3. Fold the box along the vertical score line. Reinforce the fold by using firm strokes up and down the fold with the flat surface of the bone folder. This is the spine of the outer case.

4. Place the folded box on top of the paper cutter. The spine should be on the left side. Align the spine along the vertical 7-inch mark. Cut off excess box on the right side.

5. Turn the folded box so that the spine is on the top. Push down the box so the bottom is firmly along the bottom edge of the paper cutter. Move the box slightly over to the right so that only ⅛ inch or less is exposed. Cut off the excess to make a right angle between the cut edge and the top and bottom of the box.

6. Turn the folded box and push down the box so that the spine is firmly along the bottom edge of the paper cutter. Align the left edge of the folded box along the vertical 4½-inch mark. Cut off the excess box on the right side. This is the outer case.

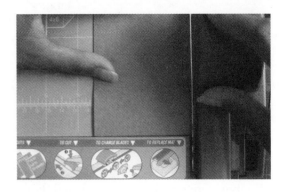

Book block

7. Since the size of the outer case measures 4½ × 7 inches, the paper in the book block should fit snugly inside. Using the paper cutter, cut the **twenty scrap sheets** down to 4½ × 6⅞. Gather them together so they form a neat pile, at least two of the edges aligning. This is your book block.

Putting it all together

8. Place the book block inside the outer case. Press the case closed with your fingers. Lift it, tapping the edges against a hard surface to en-

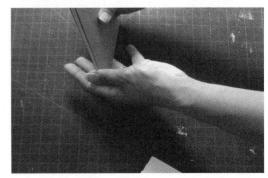

sure the case and book block are flush with each other. This is the unbound notepad.

9. Place on top of the cutting mat and put a hand weight on top to prevent it from moving. Using the awl, punch five equidistant holes vertically approximately ¾ inch from the spine. Be sure the holes go all the way through the book block as well as both sides of the case.

10. Place the unbound notepad at the edge of a table, leaving the spine hanging over the edge. Place a weight on top to prevent it from moving.

11. Thread the needle with the **string.** Starting from the back, push the threaded needle through the middle hole.

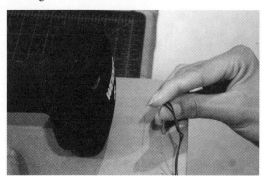

12. Follow the sewing pattern below, which is known as a "pamphlet stitch."

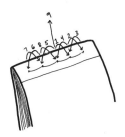

13. Add this crisscross stitch.

14. Tie the ends and cut off the excess string.

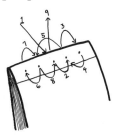

2. Rolled Magazine Bead Bracelet

MAKING BEADS by rolling up strips of magazine pages is easy enough for my seven-year-old daughter to do, yet it's sophisticated enough to not look as though a seven-year-old made it. In fact, most people will not even know that your wonderful little bracelet is a recycled gem unless you make them look—really, really close. So it's up to you: Should you be a little boastful of your talents by telling everyone in the room that you made it yourself? Or do you want to secretly enjoy the fact that you can make your own accessories to match your outfit without breaking open your piggy bank?

I choose the latter. And when I'm feeling poor (which is more often than not), I like to make these beads using magazine advertisements of expensive jewelry. So when someone asks me what kind of bracelet I'm wearing, I can cheekily say "Prada" or "Tiffany's."

Materials

2 magazine sheets
White glue
1 piece string, approximately 3 feet long
1 round button, at least ¾ inch in diameter
Glaze or varnish

Tools

Ruler   2 bamboo skewers
Pencil   Paintbrush
Paper cutter

Tips

• If you want to make a matching necklace, double the amount of beads.

• If you want to disguise the magazines completely, you can paint them with acrylic paints before adding the glaze.

Long beads

1. Using the ruler and pencil, mark ½-inch increments at the top of one **magazine sheet.** At the bottom of the sheet, mark ¼ inch from the right edge, then mark ½-inch increments thereafter.

2. Using the paper cutter, cut the sheet into long triangles. Use the marks at the top and bottom of the sheet as guides. Cut out eighteen triangles plus two or three extra for mistakes.

3. Determine which side is the front and back of the triangles.

4. Add a very thin stream of glue to the back of one triangle. Be sure to leave ¾ inch at the wide end of the triangle glue-free.

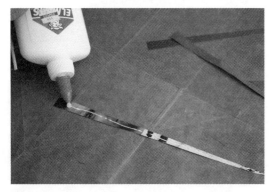

5. Starting at the wide end of the triangle, roll the triangle around one bamboo skewer. This is a long bead.

6. Repeat steps 4 and 5 until you have eighteen long beads. Brush a thin layer of varnish onto the beads and let dry for at least 3 hours.

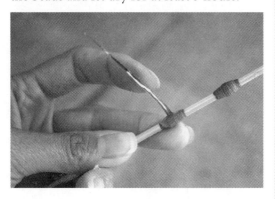

Short beads

7. Using the ruler and pencil mark ¼-inch increments at the top of magazine sheet. At the bottom of the sheet, mark the other ⅛ inch from the right edge, then mark ¼-inch increments thereafter.

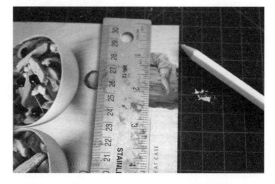

8. Using the paper cutter, cut the sheet into long triangles. Use the marks at the top and bottom of the sheet as guides. Cut out eighteen triangles plus two or three extra for mistakes.

9. Add a very thin stream of glue to the back of one triangle. Be sure to leave ¾ inch at the wide end of the triangle glue-free.

10. Starting at the wide end of the triangle, roll the triangle around the second bamboo skewer. This is a short bead.

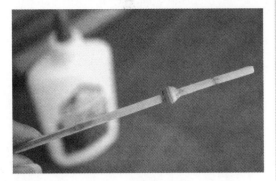

11. Repeat steps 9 and 10 until you have eighteen short beads. Brush a thin layer of varnish onto the beads and let dry for at least 3 hours.

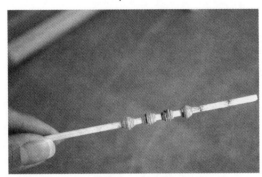

Putting it all together

12. Once both sets of beads are dry, remove them from the skewers by twisting them off.

13. Fold the piece of **string** in half, and then fold in half again. At the closed end, tie a knot so that a small loop approximately ¼ inch in di-

ameter is formed. Trim the other end so that there are four loose ends.

14. Divide the string at the loop, two strings on each side, so that there are two "legs." Add the nine short and nine long beads to one leg in an alternating manner.

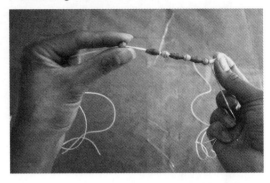

15. Add nine short and nine long beads to the other leg in an alternating manner. Take all four loose ends of the string and tie a knot.

16. Add the **button** to the loose ends, and then make a knot. Trim away the excess string, leaving approximately ¼ inch.

3. "Sock" Monkey

OKAY, THIS VERSION does not actually use a sock. In fact, unless the socks are brand new, it is probably the worst recycled material to use for making a stuffed animal. Who wants to cuddle up to some smelly old used socks that most likely have permanent stains? However, for the sake of recognizing a traditional sewing craft (let's face it—we're not reinventing the wheel), we'll just call it a "sock" monkey. The cutting pattern is still pretty much intact. If you still want to split hairs, write the publisher and give them your two cents—but don't expect your money back any time soon.

Children's knitted tights are colorful and usually not as worn as a sock at the end of its lifecycle. Most little girls grow so fast that they do not use them more than a handful of times, much to the chagrin of fashionable moms. And because the tights are on the smaller side, they make really adorable "sock" monkeys. Just ask my son's friend Molly. Her mom gave me her used knitted tights for the "sock" monkey pictured here.

Materials

1 pair children's tights
Leftover yarn or embroidery floss, about
    3 yards or 9 feet of one color
Beeswax (optional)
An old pillow (preferably with synthetic
    stuffing)
Leftover yarn or embroidery floss in red, black,
    and blue
Fabric glue

Tools

Scissors
1 thick embroidery needle
Binder clips or clothespins

Tips

- If you only have solid colored knitted tights, try pairing up different solid colors together. This will give you the ability to mix and match different colored limbs.

- You can also try bolder colors for the yarn or embroidery floss and use a blanket stitch when sewing up the body parts. (For instructions on how to do a blanket stitch, see page xvii.)

The main body and legs

1. Flatten the pair of tights in profile view. Using the scissors, cut off the legs above where the knees should be. (If you want longer limbs, cut closer to the panty section of the tights.)

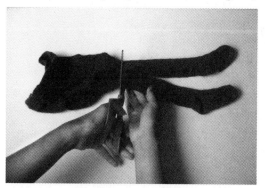

2. Set aside one of the legs. Flatten the remaining leg again so the front of the foot is on one side

and the back is on the other. Move it around so the closed toe area is at the top. Starting from the bottom, cut up the middle until about ½ inch before reaching the heel. This will be the body of the monkey.

3. Thread your thick embroidery needle with the **yarn.** You may need to use a bit of beeswax at the tip of your yarn to prevent fraying. Begin sewing the legs of the body using blanket stitch (see page xvii).

4. Cut open the pillow. As you sew the legs of the monkey's body, use the stuffing from the **pillow** to fill up the monkey. Do not wait to stuff the monkey until the end.

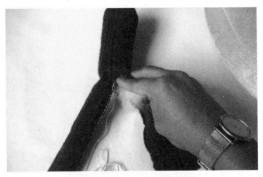

Tail, mouth, and arms

5. Take the other leg and make sure it is flattened in profile view. Cut off a strip about ½ to ¾ inch wide from the open end to the closed toe. This is the tail.

6. Cut off the heel. This is the mouth.

7. Cut off the remaining part of the leg at the ankle, and then cut in half lengthwise. These are the two arms. Discard the rest.

8. Begin sewing the tail from the closed toe end. Using the stuffing from the pillow, fill in the tail as you sew. Attach the tail to the rear end of the main monkey body.

9. Sew the mouth to the front of the main monkey body. When there is about 1 inch left to sew, fill in with the old pillow stuffing. Finish sewing the mouth.

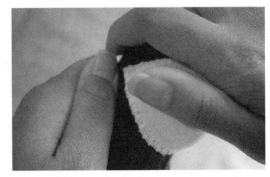

10. Sew the arms. Be sure to fill the arms with the stuffing as you sew. Attach arms to the sides of the main monkey body.

Finishing the head and face

11. To make the head appear round, pinch the area behind the mouth. Sew a few tight stitches and tie a knot.

12. To make ears, pinch the top sides of the head with binder clips or clothespins. Sew across the bottom and remove the clips. If you want to give the ears more shape, do a decorative blanket stitch on the outer edges.

13. Give the monkey a smile: pinch the mouth and sew a solid single line across using red yarn.

14. From any leftover knitted tights material, cut out two small ovals for eyes. Sew the eyes above the mouth using blue yarn. Add a little fabric glue to ensure that the eyes will not fall off.

15. To make a nose, tie a double knot at the end of your black yarn. Make a sideways pinch in the area above the smile and push the needle through once. Pull on the floss or yarn tightly and tie a double knot, holding the pinch in place. Make a few more stitches in a triangular shape.

4. Universal Little Wallet

WHO COULDN'T USE a little help organizing all that loose change jangling around in a bag or coat pocket? I know that I can. Before I figured out how to make one of these nifty little wallets, I used to carry my coins around in a snack-size plastic bag. (I'm one of those anti–large wallets people.) How unfashionable is that?

And it doesn't have to hold coins. You can use this purse to hold stamps, business cards, store coupons, or receipts. I like making a little wallet when I'm giving someone a gift card or cash as a present. I might add the recipient's initials to the front or the closing flap for a personal touch.

Materials

"The mix" (see page xvi)
1 gift bag (paper, not plastic), taken apart and
    unfolded
1 brown paper grocery bag
1 Velcro tab
1 cereal or cookie box, taken apart and
    flattened

Tools

Paper cutter   Cutting mat
1-inch-wide   Craft knife
    paintbrush   Bone folder
Long metal ruler

Tips

- If you want to be able to fit business cards in your little wallet, adjust the width of the boards from 3 to 3½ inches.
- If you don't have any old gift bags lying around, try using a poster or magazine cover.

The outer case

1. Cut the **box** in half lengthwise. Using the brush, apply a thin layer of "the mix" to one of the box pieces. Add the other box piece on top. With a bone folder, smooth down the top box piece, removing any air pockets. Allow to dry for at least 20 minutes. These are the supporting boards of the wallet.

2. Once the boards are dry, cut them into pieces using the paper cutter: two 3-inch-square pieces and one piece measuring 2 × 3 inches.

3. Spread the **gift bag** over a cutting mat with the laminated side face down. Place the metal ruler horizontally on top.

4. Take one 3-inch-square board and apply a thin layer of **"the mix"** to one side. With the glue side face down, place the board on top of the gift bag. Be sure to align one of the edges with the metal ruler. Take the second 3-inch-square board and apply a thin layer of "the mix" to one side. With the glue side face down, place the board on top of the gift bag, to the right of the first board piece and aligned with the metal ruler. Be sure that there is a ½-inch space between the two boards—this is the bottom joint.

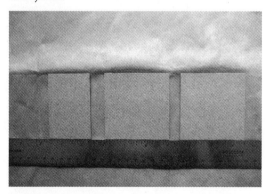

5. Take the last board piece, 2 × 3 inches. Be sure the 2-inch side is at the bottom. Apply a thin layer of "the mix" to one side. With the glue side face down, place the board on top of the gift bag, to the left of the first board piece, and

aligned with the metal ruler. Be sure that there is a ⅝-inch space between this and the first board piece—this is the top joint.

6. Quickly flip over the gift bag so the laminated side is face up. Using a bone folder, smooth down the areas where the gift bag is glued down to the board pieces, removing any air pockets.

7. Flip over the gift bag again so the boards are face up. Take the metal ruler and align it horizontally against the bottom of the three boards. Cut off the excess gift bag paper at the bottom.

8. Take the metal ruler and align it horizontally against the top of the three boards. Cut off the excess gift bag paper at the top. Do the same to the left and right sides.

9. Cut off all four corner of the gift bag paper at 45-degree angles. Leave a ⅛-inch margin at the corners of the boards.

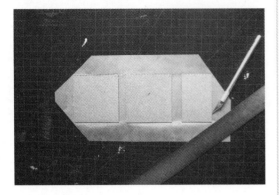

10. Place a waste sheet underneath. Apply a thin layer of "the mix" on the bottom border. Pull the waste sheet tightly up and over, which should also pull the gift bag paper over the boards.

11. Using the bone folder, smooth out the gift bag paper over the boards, eliminating any air pockets and making sharper edges.

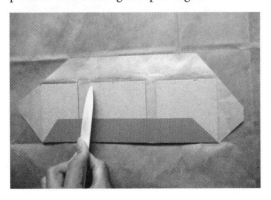

12. Repeat steps 10 and 12 on the top border as well as the left and right sides. This is the outer case.

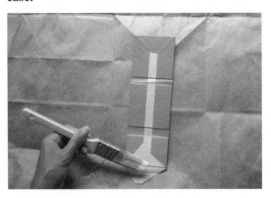

The side pieces

13. Cut two 3-inch-square pieces from the **brown paper grocery bag.** Fold each of them in half lengthwise. Fold the sides down on the diagonal, creating wings. These are the side pieces.

14. Place the side pieces, narrow tip side down, on top of the middle square of the outer case. Apply a thin layer of "the mix" to the bottom

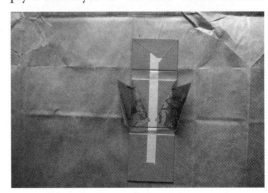

wings of each side piece and align it to the outer edges of the middle square. The narrow tip of each side piece should sit halfway in the bottom joint.

15. Apply a thin layer of "the mix" on the top wings of each side piece. Fold over the bottom square and press down firmly. This is now the unlined wallet.

Making the lining

16. Cut a piece of brown paper grocery bag 8¾ inches long × 2¾ inches high. Measure and mark down 3 inches along the bottom edge. Fold paper vertically at the 2¾-inch mark. This is the lining.

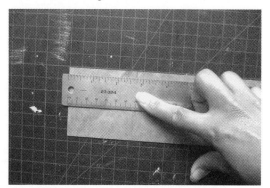

17. Unfold paper and apply a thin layer of the mix to one side. Insert the lining into the wallet, creased end first. With the bone folder, smooth down the lining against the inside of the wallet.

18. Remove one of the safety backings from the Velcro tabs and place inside the top of the change purse. Remove the other safety backing and use to close the top of the wallet.

5. Cardboard House

IF YOUR DAUGHTER is like mine, a prefab dollhouse is not going to cut it. Building your own dollhouse allows your little girl to be both interior decorator and architect. All you need depending on your little architect's blueprints are a few corrugated boxes. You can go to your local grocery store for the boxes or, if you are like me and love to shop at Amazon.com, you can slowly save up your boxes.

And if you have a son who might get a little green with envy over the dollhouse construction, you can make him a car garage using the same set of instructions. All you need to do is add a ramp. Oh, and make sure to avoid any pink in your decorating scheme.

Materials

2 (at least) corrugated boxes
Tacky glue
Acrylic paints
Cork board or towel
2 sheets thick colored paper, from a used
    school folder
Thin cotton fabric (from an old T-shirt or
    blouse)
Fabric glue
String, at least 10 inches per set of window
    curtains

Tools

Craft knife   Paper cutter
Metal ruler   Paintbrush

Tips

- Before you begin, measure the dolls that will be used with the house. Make sure they will fit inside.

- When decorating the walls and cutting out the windows, make sure you do so to scale as much as possible.

Creating the house structure

1. Be sure to clean the boxes with a slightly damp sponge. With **tacky glue,** glue the bottom of each box closed. Be sure the flaps of the bottom inside the box are touching. Add a hand weight to hold the flaps in place while the glue dries.

2. Once the glue is dried, cut off one of the top flaps of each box. Set aside one of the flaps.

3. Stack the boxes so that the sides with the flaps cut off are touching one another. Glue the boxes together. This is the main body of the house, with a first and second floor.

4. On the left and right walls of each floor, cut out 3-inch squares as close to the center as possible. These are the windows.

5. Take the cut-off flap from step 2. Fold it into a triangle and glue it together. Allow time for the glue to dry before proceeding to the next step.

6. Place the triangle on top of the main body of the house. Be sure that the edge is flush with the house. Glue it down.

7. Push over the top flap of the house so that it touches the triangle. Glue it down. This is the roof.

Adding the details

8. Paint the inside of the house with acrylic paints.

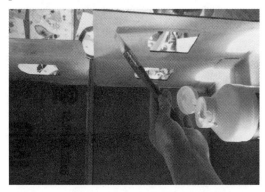

9. Measure the floors of the house. Cut up the **cork** and use to cover up the floors.

10. Using the paper cutter, cut the **colored paper** into 2 × 1-inch rectangles. Glue them on top of the roof, alternating the colors.

11. Cut up the **fabric** into eight 4 × 6½-inch rectangles.

12. Divide the rectangles into pairs, and sew them loosely together at the top. These are the curtains for the windows.

13. Use the **fabric glue** to attach the rectangles to the window, two per window.

14. Tie back the curtains with the string. Use five inches of string per curtain.

February

Projects This Month:

LOVE Embroidered Card

Keepsake Box

Paper Dolls

Envelopes

DESPITE ITS BREVITY, February is big on celebrations and offers something for everyone. From Mardi Gras to No Brainer Day, the mere act of waking up in the morning is a reason to party. But we all know, of course, which day we are really looking forward to and, no, it's not Pistol Patent Day.

All things red and pink, however nauseating they may be the rest of the year, somehow captures our imagination for twenty eight days (twenty nine each Leap Year). And we love . . . anything corny, anything schmaltzy, and anything that is annoyingly too cute. We love the idea of LOVE, which may explain why February is the shortest month of the year. Because the pursuit of love is simply too exhausting.

Materials you will need this month

1 white cardboard insert (plain T-shirt or bedding packaging)

Craft glue stick

1 old handkerchief or T-shirt (100% cotton)

Leftover embroidery floss

Fabric glue

Waxed paper

1 cereal box

1 gift bag (paper, not plastic)

1 half-gallon juice or milk carton

1 brown paper grocery bag

"The mix" (see page xvi)

1 corrugated box

Yarn or embroidery floss

Buttons

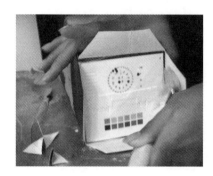

Old greeting cards (winter holiday, birthday, etc.)
Magazine sheets
Used wrapping paper

February holidays, typical and not-so

Groundhog Day (2nd)

Disaster Day (5th)

Mardi Gras (a Tuesday, but changes every year—sometimes it's in January)

Umbrella Day (10th)

Chinese New Year (a.k.a. Lunar New Year—this changes every year)

White T-shirt Day (11th)

Get a Different Name Day (13th)

St. Valentine's Day (14th)

Presidents' Day (3rd Monday)

National Battery Day (February 18th)

National Chocolate Mint Day (19th)

International Dog Biscuit Appreciation Day (23rd)

International Polar Bear Day (27th)

Public Sleeping Day (28th)

National Surf 'n' Turf Day (29th)

Monthlong celebrations

American Heart Month

American History Month

Black History Month

National Blah Buster Month

National Cherry Month

Children's Dental Health Month

National Embroidery Month

International Friendship Month

National Grapefruit Month

National Snack Food Month

National Weddings Month

Responsible Pet Owner Month

Return Carts to the Supermarket Month

Creative Romance Month

International Twit Award Month

National Wild Bird Feeding Month

Canned Food Month

February birthdays of famous people

Langston Hughes (2nd)

Ayn Rand (2nd)

Norman Rockwell (3rd)

Betty Friedan (4th)

Rosa Parks (4th)

Hank Aaron (5th)

Ronald Reagan (6th)

Babe Ruth (6th)

Thomas Edison (11th)

Abraham Lincoln (12th)

Charles Darwin (12th)

Susan B. Anthony (15th)

George Washington (22nd)

Johnny Cash (26th)

John Steinbeck (27th)

Henry Wadsworth Longfellow (27th)

6. LOVE Embroidered Card

EMBROIDERY IS NOT just for pillows. In fact, you can embroider just about anything—that is, anything that isn't a metal and at least ¼ inch thick. Or *can* you? Hmm.

In the past, I've made this card for baby showers or a child's first birthday. It makes a great keepsake that you can frame or convert into a door knocker.

Materials

1 white cardboard insert (plain T-shirt or bedding packaging)
Craft glue stick
1 old handkerchief or T-shirt (100% cotton)
Leftover embroidery floss
Fabric glue

Tools

Thick embroidery needle	Metal ruler
Beeswax	Pencil
Scissors	Bone folder
Paper cutter	Sheet of waxed paper, at least 7 × 6 inches
Awl	Craft knife

Tips

- A thin 100% cotton fabric works best for this type of craft project. Try ironing your material first before gluing it to the cardboard.

- For a more quiltlike appearance, you can add a sheet of paper towel between the cardboard and fabric.

The base card

1. Using the paper cutter, cut a 5½ × 8-inch rectangle from the **cardboard.** Fold in half to 5½ × 4½ inches. This is your base card.

Drawing the design

2. Position the base card in the landscape format, with the card opening at the bottom. The top of the card is the front panel. With the pencil and the ruler, draw an inner border approximately ¼ inch from the outer perimeter of the front panel. Write the word "Love" in the center of the front panel. This is the design.

3. Using the awl, gently punch holes over the design. Be sure to space the holes ¼ inch apart.

4. Apply a thin layer of glue with the craft glue stick and place the **handkerchief** on top. Smooth out any air pockets by gently rubbing the bone folder over the surface.

5. Trim away any excess fabric at the edges of the front panel. Be sure to leave a little extra fabric about ⅛ inch all around the front panel.

The stitching

6. Thread the needle with **embroidery floss.** Starting from the back side of the front panel, begin stitching the design.

7. To find the second hole to continue stitching, poke a hole through it from the back side of the front panel with the needle. Then push the needle through from the front side.

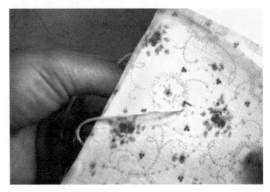

8. From this point on, you will always advance your stitches, starting from the back side and going toward the front side. Conversely, when you finish a stitch, you will always backtrack one stitch, going from the front side to the back side.

9. When you are done stitching the design, tie a knot and cut off any excess floss.

10. Using the craft knife and metal ruler trim off the excess fabric at the edges. Be sure the card is closed. To get a clean cut it may be necessary to trim off a bit of the cardboard on the three open sides.

sure to do this while the card is open so you do not glue the card shut by accident.

12. Place a piece of waxed paper inside the card and allow the fabric glue to dry overnight.

11. Add a little fabric glue to the edges of the front panel to prevent the cloth from fraying. Be

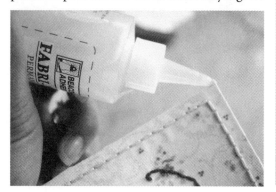

7. Keepsake Box

I ADMIT THAT I am addicted to making these boxes. In my closet, I have at least four boxes to use for emergency gifts. To personalize them, I simply embroider a small piece of cardboard and glue it to the top of the box. I'll place a small gift inside (jewelry for a girl, maybe a wallet or money holder for a boy) and then wrap it with a satin ribbon.

These boxes are also good to keep things organized on top of any dresser. My daughter has tons of ponytail holders, headbands, bracelets, and other accessories that would drive any sane parent to the edge. I've made her a few of these boxes and she now keeps her stuff more or less organized.

Materials

"The mix" (see page xvi)
1 cereal box
1 gift bag (paper, not plastic)
1 half-gallon juice or milk carton
1 brown paper grocery bag

Tools

Paper cutter	Metal ruler
Waste sheets	1-inch-wide
Bone folder	paintbrush
Craft knife	Small hand weights

Tip

- Making boxes can be a sticky mess. To prevent the components from sticking to each other when they are *not* supposed to, have a good supply of waste sheets on hand. Remove them often to maintain a clean and glue-free working surface.

Preparing the boards

1. Take apart the **cereal box** at the glued seams. Cut in half so that the front and back panels of the box are intact.

2. Place on top of waste sheets. Apply a thin layer of **"the mix"** on the surface of one box panel. Be sure to cover the entire surface evenly.

3. Place the other box panel on top of the first box panel. Smooth out any air pockets by gently but firmly rubbing the bone folder over the surface. Allow "the mix" to dry for a few minutes.

4. Using a paper cutter, cut the box panels into two 4¼ × 4⅛-inch rectangles and one 4¼ × 3-inch rectangle. These are the boards.

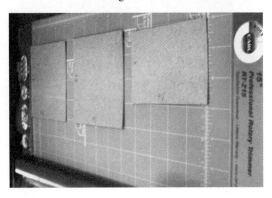

The casing

5. Take the **gift bag** apart at the glued seams. Place it, printed side down, on top of the waste sheets. Place a metal ruler across the bottom edge of the gift bag.

6. Apply a thin layer of "the mix" on one of the boards. Place it, glue side down, on top of the gift bag. Be sure to align the 4⅛-inch bottom side with the edge of the ruler.

7. Apply a thin layer of "the mix" to the other two boards. Place them glue side down on top of the gift bag, with the smaller board in the middle. The height of all three boards should be 4¼ inches. Leave a ⅛-inch space between the boards. Turn over and smooth out any air pockets by gently rubbing the bone folder over the surface.

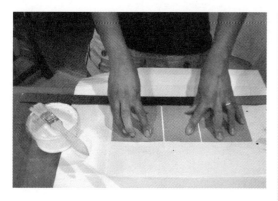

8. Cut off any excess gift bag around the boards, leaving an approximately 1-inch border of gift bag around the perimeter of the boards.

9. Cut off the four corners of the border at 45-degree angles approximately ¹⁄₁₆ inch from the corners of the boards.

10. Apply a thin layer of "the mix" to the bottom edge. Pull the waste sheet underneath up and over the boards. Smooth out any air pockets with the bone folder.

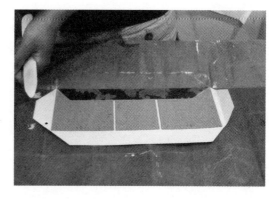

11. Repeat step 10 on the other three sides. This is the casing of the box.

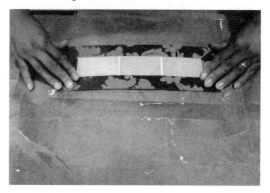

The base

12. Use the craft knife to cut out the bottom portion of the milk carton. Be sure that it is 3 inches tall all around.

13. You will need at least an 8 × 15½-inch piece of gift bag paper to cover the milk carton. Place the gift bag paper printed side down on top of the waste sheets. Apply a thin layer of

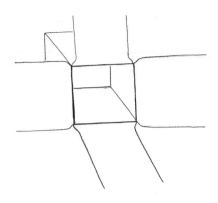

"the mix" on the gift bag paper. Place the milk carton on top. Align one vertical edge of milk carton with the vertical left edge of the gift bag paper and leave an approximately 1-inch space at the bottom. Roll the milk carton over the gift bag paper. As you roll one side, smooth out any air pockets with the bone folder before continuing on to the next side. Cut off any excess gift bag paper once you have completely covered all four sides.

14. Turn milk carton on its side so that the bottom is facing you. Pinch one of the corners and cut off at a 45-degree angle. Repeat on each corner. Cut the corner of the bottom at a 45-degree angle. Glue down flaps to bottom of the milk carton.

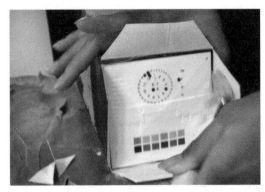

15. Turn the milk carton so that the open end faces you. Cut slits into the gift bag paper at the four corners, but make sure that the cuts are slightly wide. See diagram.

16. Glue down the top flaps of the gift bag paper to the inside of the milk carton. Each flap should be longer than the sides of the milk carton and should partially cover the inside bottom. This is the base of the box.

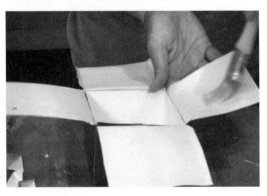

17. Apply a thin layer of "the mix" to the bottom of the base. Place the base on top of one of the rectangles of the casing. Be sure the base sits flush against the joint of the casing. Place a hand weight inside the base and let "the mix" dry for an hour.

18. While "the mix" is drying, cut out a 4 × 5-inch rectangle and a 3-inch square from the **brown paper grocery bag.**

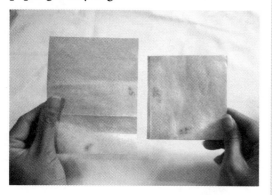

19. After an hour has passed, remove the hand weight. Apply a thin layer of "the mix" to the brown paper grocery bag square and place it, glue side down, inside the base.

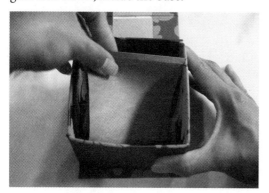

20. Apply a thin layer of "the mix" to the bag rectangle and place it, glue side down, on the casing. Be sure to center it to the top of the casing.

21. Apply a thin layer of "the mix" to the center rectangle of the casing and press it against the side of the base. Place between two hardcover books and put a hand weight on top. Let it sit overnight.

8. Paper Dolls

THIS IS AN OLDIE BUT GOODIE. When I was a little girl, paper dolls were something of an immediate gratification. Although the dolls themselves were part of a kit, the dresses and accessories were something that I could draw, color, and cut out myself. It was an inexpensive alternative to actual dolls, and also encouraged my creative side. Sometimes the outfits were made from scraps of cloth rather than paper. As long as I could cut something with a pair of scissors, then it was a viable material for paper doll clothing.

I've passed on the tradition of do-it-yourself paper dolls to my daughter, who sometimes uses pieces of cloth that, well, are not quite yet scraps. So the only warning you might want to give your child is to *not* use something that is not quite ready for the recycle bin! That is, unless you want to find holes in your curtains or tablecloth.

Materials

1 corrugated box
Yarn or embroidery floss
Buttons
Old greeting cards (winter holiday, birthday, etc.)
Magazine sheets
White glue

Tools

Scissors
Pencil
Set of multicolor markers

Tip

- To give the paper dolls a longer shelf life, glue a chopstick or Popsicle stick to the back. This will give additional support to the neck, which usually begins to flop over after a few sessions of play.

    1. Photocopy the template provided *at 200 percent,* and trace two paper dolls onto a piece of corrugated cardboard.

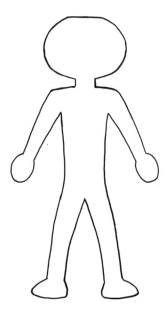

2. Carefully cut out the dolls.

3. Use yarn or embroidery floss for hair by cutting it into smaller pieces and glue onto the top of the doll's head. For a girl, use 5-inch strips. For a boy (depending on how shaggy you want his hair to be), use 1-inch strips.

4. Buttons can be used for many things. Small buttons approximately ¼ inch in diameter can be used for eyes. Larger ones can be used for closures on blouses or oxford shirts on the doll.

5. Old greeting cards and magazines provide lots of patterns and textures for doll clothing. Once you find a pattern or texture that you like, place the doll on top and lightly trace the outline with a pencil.

6. When all else fails, markers or paints can be used to clothe your paper doll. Or use them to add finishing touches, like facial features.

9. Envelopes

OKAY, THIS IS NOT QUITE A CRAFT. But how many times have you searched high and low for an envelope, only to realize that you haven't bought any, because you do everything online these days? In this day and age, when we can pay our bills online or write someone an e-mail in lieu of snail mail, envelopes have become almost a thing of the past.

But hang on. Sometimes you need to send out a card—yes, an actual card!—to a loved one because you missed a birthday and an impersonal e-mail just won't do. Or some antiquated company does not offer online payment services, so you really do need to mail in that payment. Ugh.

Well, here are two envelope sizes that you will most likely need: the business size (4⅛ × 9½ inches) and the greeting card size (5¾ × 4⅜ inches). (You can thank me later.)

Materials

Magazine sheets and other large pieces of scrap paper no smaller than 8½ × 11 inches
Glue stick

Tools

Pencil
Scissors or craft knife

Tip

- Keep a running supply of white labels to be used for writing down addresses. Then you can use any magazine or catalog sheet—regardless of how dark or colorful it is—as an envelope.

1. Photocopy the templates on the next page *at 200 percent.*

2. Cut out each template along the solid line.

3. Trace on top of desired paper, and cut out envelope shape.

4. Add glue on the edges to ensure your letter or card doesn't fall out.

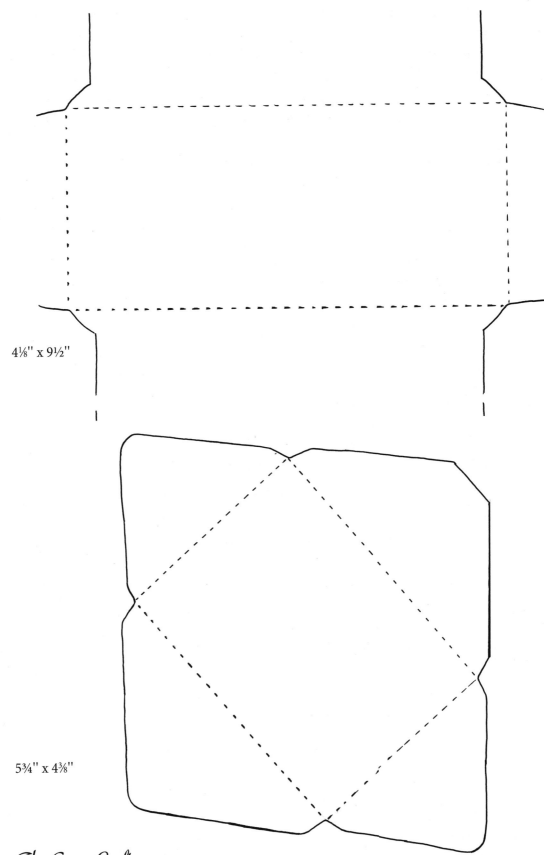

4⅛" x 9½"

5¾" x 4⅜"

March

Projects This Month

Your Basic Diamond Kite
Indoor Window Planter
String Puppet
Milk Carton Toy Boat

MARCH. IT IS MORE OF AN ORDER than the name of a month. And, oh, you better march! It's a word that encapsulates something simple yet powerful, a monosyllabic force that tells you to move on and don't look back. It's cold and dark back there, so keep going until the warm weather comes.

Because it's coming. With daylight savings and the start of spring (and not to mention the start of the baseball season), it's not too early to pick out a new bathing suit . . . okay, maybe it's too early for a bathing suit. But, hey, a short-sleeved shirt is not out of the question, although I'd still dress in layers if I were you.

Oh, just march.

Materials you will need this month

6 bamboo barbecue skewers, 12 inches long
Colored duct tape
10 large paper clips
1 plastic grocery bag
1 plastic bread or newspaper bag
At least 10 feet of string wound around an empty toilet paper
    roll, plus an additional 7 feet
3 half-gallon milk or juice cartons
Cellophane tape
Fabric glue
1 hard plastic rectangular produce container
Twine, approximately 20 feet or more
Potting soil
1 plastic bottle, approximately 2½ inches in diameter, 4½ inches tall, with a
    screw cap

1 Ping-Pong ball

1 large bead

Yarn

Fabric glue

2 plastic round bottle caps, approximately 1½ inches in diameter

2 large round buttons

1 old scarf

Thread

Ribbon, 12 inches long

1 pair chopsticks

1 thick/retail plastic bag, (e.g., store bag)

Artist's tape

March holidays, typical and not-so

National Pig Day (1st)

National Anthem Day (3rd)

National Frozen Food Day (6th)

International Women's Day (8th)

Daylight saving time begins
(2nd Sunday)

Festival of Life in the Cracks Day
(10th)

Jewel Day (13th)

National Potato Chip Day (14th)

Everything You Do Is Right Day (16th)

St. Patrick's Day (17th)

First Day of Spring (20th/21st)

National Goof-off Day (22nd)

National Chocolate Covered Raisins
Day (24th)

Pecan Day and Waffle Day (25th)

National "Joe" Day (27th)

National Clams on the Half Shell Day
(31st)

Monthlong celebrations

American Red Cross Month

Foot Health Month

Humorists Are Artist Month

Irish-American Heritage Month

Music in our Schools Month

National Craft Month

National Furniture Refinishing Month

National Frozen Food Month

National Noodle Month

National Peanut Month

Woman's History Month

Youth Art Month

March birthdays of famous people

March birthdays of famous people

Dr. Seuss (2nd)

Alexander Graham Bell (3rd)

Elizabeth Barret Browning (6th)

Albert Einstein (14th)

Grover Cleveland (18th)

Fred Rogers (20th)

Harry Houdini (24th)

Sandra Day O'Connor (26th)

Tennessee Williams (26th)

Robert Frost (26th)

Gloria Steinem (25th)

Cy Young (29th)

Al Gore (31st)

10. Your Basic Diamond Kite

THERE ARE A LOT of different kites out there, but the one that seems to hold a nostalgic place in everyone's heart is this diamond kite. It's simple to make and, yes, really does fly high (well, depending on the size of the open field and what aerobic shape you are in). And is it really that much more windy in the month of March than any other month? No, not really. I think it's more of a symbolic gesture, that we should go outdoors, run around like maniacs, and yank a piece of plastic tied to some sticks. We've been indoors for months and months, so it really does make sense.

Materials

4 bamboo barbecue skewers, 12 inches long

Colored duct tape

1 paper clip

1 thick plastic bag (from a retail store), cut at seams to form one flat piece

1 plastic bread or newspaper bag

At least 10 feet of string wound around an empty toilet paper roll (see Tip)

Tools

Chain-nose pliers

Round-nose pliers

Protractor

Scissors

Thick tapestry needle

Tip

- To prevent the string from falling off the toilet paper roll, slightly crush the tube in the center before rolling the string around it.

The frame

1. Align the two **bamboo skewers** on a horizontal plane with the pointed ends facing in towards each other. Using the **duct tape,** connect the two skewers in the middle.

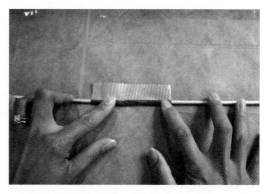

2. Unwind the **paper clip** to make a straight line. Using the chain-nose and round-nose pliers,

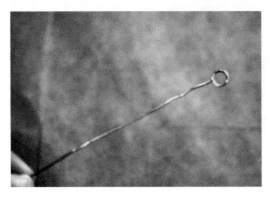

twist one end of the paper clip to form a closed loop approximately ¼ inch in diameter. The loop should overlap itself.

3. Push one of the bamboo skewers through the paper clip loop. Bend the skewer at the taped middle so that it forms an approximate 140-degree angle. Twist the loose ends of the paper clip around the bent bamboo skewer to hold it in place.

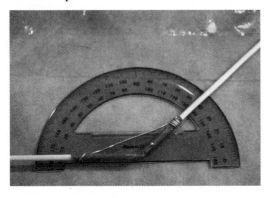

4. There should be a small opening between the paper clip and the bend between the taped

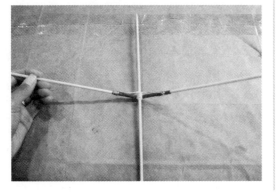

bamboo skewers. Insert a third bamboo skewer into the opening until it is halfway through. Tie it in place with the string.

5. At the pointed end of the third bamboo skewer, position and tape the pointed end of the fourth skewer. Be sure that the skewers overlap at least 2 inches and that the tape covers all the pointed ends. This is the frame.

The sail

6. Place the frame on top of the flattened plastic grocery bag so that the left and right points are face down. With a marker, lightly draw a diamond around the frame. Cut out the diamond. This is the sail.

7. Flip over the frame so that the left and right points are facing up. Tape the sail to the four points of the frame. Flip the main body of the kite so that the frame is covered by the sail.

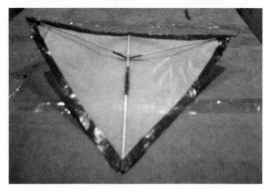

8. **String.** Cut four pieces of string, each measuring 20 inches long. Thread the needle with one of the pieces of string. Sew the string to one of the sail's points and tie a knot around the frame, being sure to leave a tail of string that measures at least 16 inches long.

9. Repeat step 8 on the remaining three points of the sail.

10. Thread a needle with the string that is wound around the toilet paper roll. Sew the string to the middle cross of the frame and tie a knot. Do *not* cut the string.

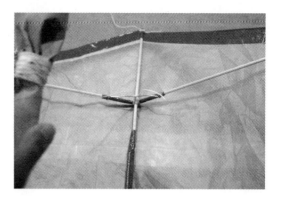

11. Hold the kite by the middle cross of the frame so that all the strings are hanging down. Tie all five strings together in the center.

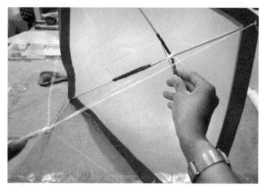

The tail

12. Take the bread bag and cut off the closed end. To yield one long piece that is approximately 1½ inches wide, cut the bag in a spiral.

13. Fold the plastic from the bag in half. Tie it to the long end of the frame. This is the tail.

14. Tie decorative bows along the tail.

11. Indoor Window Planter

IF YOU ARE LOOKING to spruce up your windows with some plants or to get a head start on your outdoor garden, these window planters are for you.

For this project, I like to save half gallon cartons that have some design to them, which I can then incorporate into the overall look of the craft. In the sample window planter below, I used half-gallon milk cartons from Trader Joe's, which have a farm scene printed on them.

Materials

2 half-gallon milk or juice cartons
Cellophane tape
Fabric glue
1 hard plastic rectangular produce container
Twine, approximately 20 feet or more
Potting soil

Tools

Fine-point marker   Craft knife
Metal ruler   Awl

Tips

• Be sure the hard plastic produce containers do not have holes in them. They will catch any excess water that flows out of the planter.

• Looking for seedlings? Try saving seeds from an apple, orange, or avocado. Place them in a clear closable plastic bag with a wet paper towel and leave it in the sun. In a few days, roots should sprout and you can transfer these seedlings into your planter.

• If you are not particularly fond of the printed graphics on the carton, you can use acrylic paint to cover it. First prime the surface with gesso.

The base

1. Cut off the top portions of the **half-gallon cartons,** leaving 4½ inches in height from the bottom.

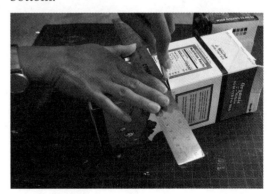

2. Tape the boxes together at the center. This is the base of the window planter.

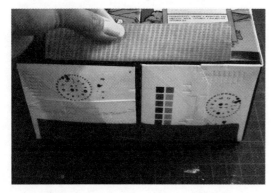

Making the top border

3. Add a dab of glue to the corner of one top. Take one end of the twine and place it on top of the glue. Carefully start winding the twine around the tops of the cartons, adding glue between the twine and the carton as you go along.

4. Wind the twine around the top so that you have ten full rows of twine. Gently push the rows together so they are taut and that the top row slightly rises over the top of the cartons.

5. Cut off the excess twine and be sure to glue down the end securely. If possible, try to tuck it into the row above it. This is the top border.

The bottom border

6. Turn the cartons upside down. Add a dab of glue to the corner. Take one end of the twine and place it on top of the glue. Carefully start winding the twine around the bottom of the cartons, adding glue between the twine and the carton as you go along.

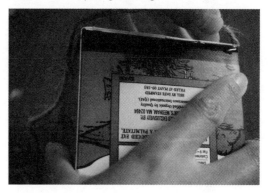

7. Wind the twine around the bottom so that you have ten full rows of twine. Gently push down the rows together so they are taut and that the last row is flush with the bottom of the carton.

8. Cut off the excess twine and be sure to glue down the end securely. If possible, try to tuck it into the row above it. This is the bottom border.

Decorating the top border

9. Cut three pieces of twine, each one 4 inches long.

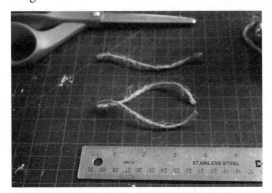

10. Turn the window planter right side up. Add glue to the middle of the top border. Take one of the 4-inch pieces of twine and form a sideways *S* on top of the glue.

11. Add glue to the left and right sides. Take the remaining two pieces of 4-inch twine and form sideways *S*'s on top of the glue.

The last touches

12. Turn the window planter upside down. Using the awl, puncture at least 6 holes in the bottom. Try to space them evenly from each other.

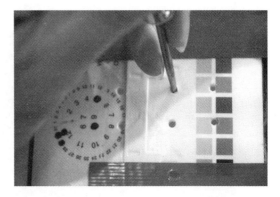

13. Turn the window planter right side up. Add your **potting soil** and seeds or seedlings. Be

sure to leave about 1 inch of space at the top of the planter.

14. Cut the lid off the **produce container.** Place the window planter inside.

12. String Puppet

HOWDY DOODY, Kukla and Ollie, and, more recently, that rascally bunch from the *Team America: World Police* movie—these are all examples of string puppets that we may remember (and possibly want to forget) from the last half of the twentieth century. They are usually made from wood or ceramic, but how about a Ping-Pong ball, a plastic bottle, and some wine corks?

Materials

9 large paper clips
1 Ping-Pong ball
1 large bead
2 plastic round bottle caps, approximately 1½ inches in diameter
8 wine corks (real cork or plastic cork)
1 plastic bottle, approximately 2½ inches in diameter, 4½ inches tall, with a screw cap
1 pair chopsticks
2 large round buttons
String, 7 feet long
Yarn
Fabric glue
1 old scarf
Ribbon, 12 inches long
Thread

Tools

Round-nose pliers   Thick tapestry needle
Chain-nose pliers   Regular sewing needle
Awl
Set of permanent
   markers, various colors

Tip

- This project requires that you push a paper clip through a cork—over and over again. While there may be one or two of you who possess enormous strength in the upper digits of your fingers, the majority of us mere mortals will find this task easier to accomplish by using a pair of chain-nose pliers.

Attaching the limbs

1. Using an awl, poke four holes (two top, two bottom) in the **plastic bottle,** to attach the arms and legs to. Be sure the bottle is right side up (cap on top) and that the holes are level and equidistant to each other. Poke a fifth hole in the center of the cap on top of the bottle.

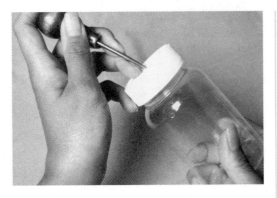

2. Using the chain-nose pliers, unwind and straighten all nine **paper clips.** Set aside five of them.

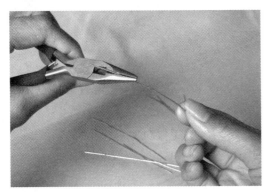

3. Using the round-nose pliers, make a closed loop approximately ¼ inch in diameter at the end of each of the four straightened paper clips.

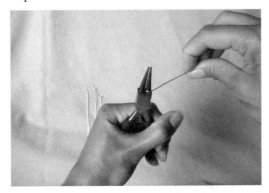

4. Take the cap off the plastic bottle and set it aside. From the inside out, insert one paper clip in each of the four holes of the plastic bottle. These are the puppet's arms.

5. Using the awl, poke holes at each end of the corks. Push one **cork** through each straightened end of the paper clips attached to the plastic bottle. Using the round-nose pliers, make a closed loop approximately ¼ inch in diameter at the end of each paper clip.

6. Using an awl, poke holes at each end of the remaining four corks. Take four of the straightened paper clips. (There should be one remaining clip; set aside.) Push one paper clip through each of the corks. These are the puppet's legs.

7. Take one of the lower limbs. Slip one end of the paper clip through the loop of one of the upper limbs. Using the round-nose pliers, make a closed loop approximately ¼ inch in diameter, attaching the lower limb to the upper limb. Repeat three more times until all four legs are attached to the the arms.

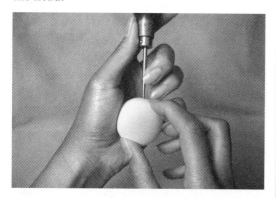

The head

8. Using the awl, poke one hole in the Ping-Pong ball and another at its opposite pole. This is the head.

9. Using permanent markers, draw a face on the head.

10. Add hair to the head by gluing on the **yarn** with **fabric glue.**

11. Starting from the top of the Ping-Pong ball, push the remaining straightened paper clip through the head. Add the bead to the wire extending from the bottom of the head. This is the neck.

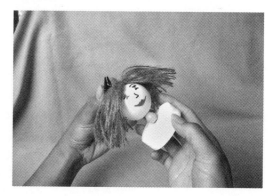

12. Using the round-nose pliers, make a closed loop approximately ¼ inch in diameter with the exposed paper clip at the top of the head. Take the cap of the plastic bottle. From the

outside in, push the exposed paper clip at the bottom of the head through the hole in the center of the cap. Make a closed loop approximately ¼ inch in diameter with the portion of the paper clip inside the cap.

13. Screw the cap back on top of the plastic bottle.

The feet and hands

14. Using the awl, poke a hole in the center of each cap. These are the feet.

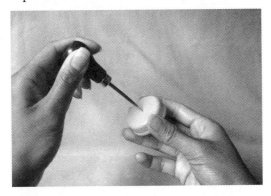

15. Take one foot. Take the lower limb of one leg and push the exposed paper clip end through

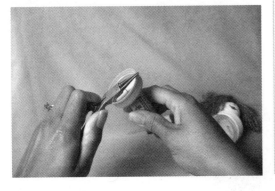

the center hole of the foot (from the outside in). Using the round-nose pliers, attach the foot by making a closed loop approximately ¼ inch in diameter on the inside of the foot. Repeat step so that both feet are attached to the lower limbs of the legs.

16. Take the lower limb of one arm and push the exposed paper clip end through one of the holes in one **button.** Using the round-nose pliers, attach the hand by making a closed loop approximately ¼ inch in diameter. Repeat with the second button so that both hands are attached to the lower limbs of the arms.

The dress

17. Fold the scarf in half and fold again into quarters. Arrange in a diamond shape, with the open edges at the bottom and the closed corner at the top. Cut off the top corner, about a ¼ inch. Unfold scarf. You should have a small rectangle in the middle of your scarf big enough to push the head of the puppet through.

18. Take each of the four corners and bring to the center hole. Using the sewing needle and thread, sew the corners so they stay in place.

19. Fold the sides in toward the middle and loosely sew it in place. This is the puppet dress.

20. Put the dress on the puppet by pushing the head through the rectangular hole.

21. Tie the ribbon around the middle of the puppet's body. Adjust the shoulders of the dress so that the arms of the puppet can move freely.

Attaching the handle

22. Arrange the **chopsticks** in a T. Use enough string to tie the chopsticks securely in place. This is the handle.

23. Cut the loose string so that a tail measuring approximately 8 inches long remains attached to the handle. Tie a knot with the end of the tail to the top loop of the puppet's head.

24. Hang the puppet from the handle so that the feet lie flat on the ground. Tie string to the hands and feet. Tie the loose ends of each string to each end of the handle. Make sure that the stings do not have any slack. Your string puppet is complete.

13. Milk Carton Toy Boat

I'VE TRIED TO make boats out of all kinds of materials: water bottles, plastic containers, Styrofoam cups, aluminum cans, and good ole paper. But this one is the best one I've made so far (if I say so myself). It looks like a sailboat rather than like something floating in the water that functions as a boat but still looks like garbage. And because it's so simple to make, you can make two, three, or four at a time. You can make a whole fleet of sailboats and race them around your swimming pool.

Materials

1 half-gallon milk or juice carton
Fabric glue
2 bamboo skewers
1 sturdy plastic bag, (e.g., department store bag)
1 wine cork
Artist's white tape

Tools

Craft knife
Cutting mat
Awl

Metal ruler
Fine-point black marker

Tip

- Try adding some extra corks on the side for buoys. It also helps keep the boat afloat just in case it's carrying a heavy load.

The boat

1. Carefully take apart the **half-gallon carton** along the seams, using the craft knife when

needed. Flatten it out over a cutting mat, un-printed side facing up.

2. Cut off the excess parts of the carton, as shown in the picture below.

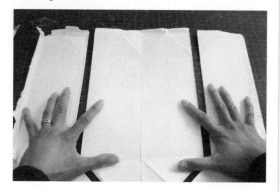

3. Glue the front end using **fabric glue,** making sure that the unprinted side is on the outside.

4. Glue the back end. This is the boat.

The sail

5. Lay one of the **bamboo skewers** flat on your worktable with the pointed end at the bottom. Take the second skewer and lay it across the first skewer approximately 3 inches from the pointed end.

6. Secure the skewers in place by tying string at the intersection. Add a little fabric glue if needed.

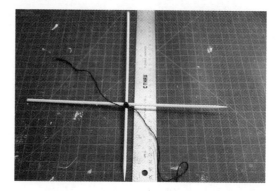

7. Cut a piece of the **plastic bag** large enough to cover the skewers. Place the piece of plastic on top of the cutting mat and then lay the skewers on top of the plastic.

8. Cut a triangle approximately ½ inch larger than the top three ends of the skewers. Discard the excess plastic.

9. Using the artist's tape, tape the ends of the triangle to the corresponding ends of the skewers. Be sure that the plastic hangs loosely from the skewers. This is your sail.

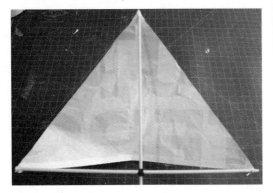

Putting it all together

10. Poke a hole in the side of the **wine cork.** It does not have to puncture the cork all the way through.

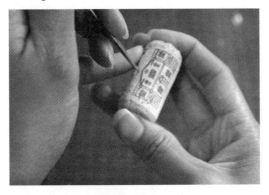

11. Glue the cork to the inside of the boat, toward the front end. Be sure the hole is facing up. Allow the glue to dry for a few hours.

12. Once the glue is dry, insert the pointed end of the sail in the hole in the cork.

13. Test the boat by allowing it to float in a bucket or basin of water. If the boat tips over, place a few small rocks inside the boat.

14. Once you get the right amount of weight inside the boat to ensure that it will not tip over, you are ready to take your boat to a larger body of water to test the sail.

April

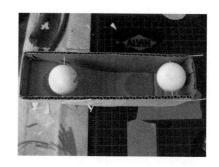

Projects This Month

Mack's Toy Car

Picture Perfect Mobile

Spare Parts Bear Doll

Cherry Blossom Greeting Card

APRIL IS THE MONTH when things get a little more interesting. Oh, sure, my friends and family would accuse me of bias just because I happen to be born in the month of April. (My birthday coincides with National Eggs Benedict Day, if anyone is wondering.) But what month can claim to celebrate poetry and yet have a day dedicated to the cheeseball? Seriously, though, April is a time when we start to see things bloom, such as the cherry blossom trees in Washington, D.C. Ah, so much beauty in the world. But wait, is that . . . that . . . aaachoo! Oh, yeah, pollen. And hay fever. And tax returns. Oh, the dreaded tax returns.

Materials you will need this month

1 piece of cardboard, no smaller than 8½ × 11 inches

2 Ping-Pong balls

4 small beads

10 large paper clips

7 school portraits, wallet size

7 playing cards or flash cards

1 wire from a used spiral notebook

Butcher string, at least 2 feet long

1 roll transparent nylon string

6 small buttons

3 trunk pieces from children's knitted tights

4 skeins embroidery floss (2 of same color, 1 black, 1 red)

1 old pillow (for stuffing) or bag of poly-fill

2 brown grocery bags

1 white cardboard insert (from T-shirt or bedding packaging)
Newspaper want ads
Pink tissue paper

April holidays, typical and not-so

April Fool's Day (1st)
National Peanut Butter and Jelly Day (2nd)
Don't Go to Work Unless It's Fun Day (3rd)
No Housework Day (7th)
Name Yourself Day (9th)
National Pecan Day (14th)
Tax Day (15th)
National Stress Awareness Day and National Eggs Benedict Day (16th)
National Cheeseball Day (17th)
International Jugglers Day (18th)
Kindergarten Day (21st)
National Jelly Bean Day (22nd)
National Pretzel Day (26th)
National Shrimp Scampi Day (29th)
National Honesty Day (30th)

Monthlong celebrations

Autism Awareness Month
International Guitar Month
Keep America Beautiful Month
National Anxiety Month
National Humor Month
National Welding Month
National Garden Month
National Frogs Month
National Poetry Month
National Child Abuse Prevention Month

April birthdays of famous people

Washington Irving (3rd)
Maya Angelou (4th)
Booker T. Washington (5th)
Butch Cassidy (6th)
Joseph Pulitzer (10th)
Thomas Jefferson (13th)
Samuel Beckett (13th)
Charlie Chaplin (16th)
Wilbur Wright (16th)
William Shakespeare (23rd)
Edward R. Murrow (25th)
Ulysses S. Grant (27th)
Samuel Morse (27th)
James Monroe (28th)
Duke Ellington (29th)
William Randolph Hearst (29th)

14. Mack's Toy Car

My son was more than thrilled to hear that I was including a toy car in this book. And not just any toy car—this particular one. I made the first one out of desperation, making my kid a toy that he could help me decorate, which is something he could not do with his Matchbox cars (no offense, but something that's 2½ inches long and made out of die-cast metal cannot easily be embellished with crayons or fat markers). But that's not the best part: this toy car has wheels that work. After decorating them, you can race them.

So this one is for you, Mack.

Materials

1 piece cardboard, no smaller than 8½ × 11 inches
White glue
Acrylic paint
2 Ping-Pong balls
4 small beads
2 large paper clips

Tools

Pencil   Round-nose pliers
Scissors   Awl
Craft knife   Paintbrush
Metal ruler   Foil tape
Bone folder

Tip

• Adding a streamer to the back will make this car extra-fun. Use the directions for a kite tail on page 33.

The main car body

1. Photocopy the template provided on page 50 *at 150 percent.* Draw or trace the outline of the unassembled body of the car on the **cardboard.** With the awl, be sure to poke holes through the cardboard where the tires will attach.

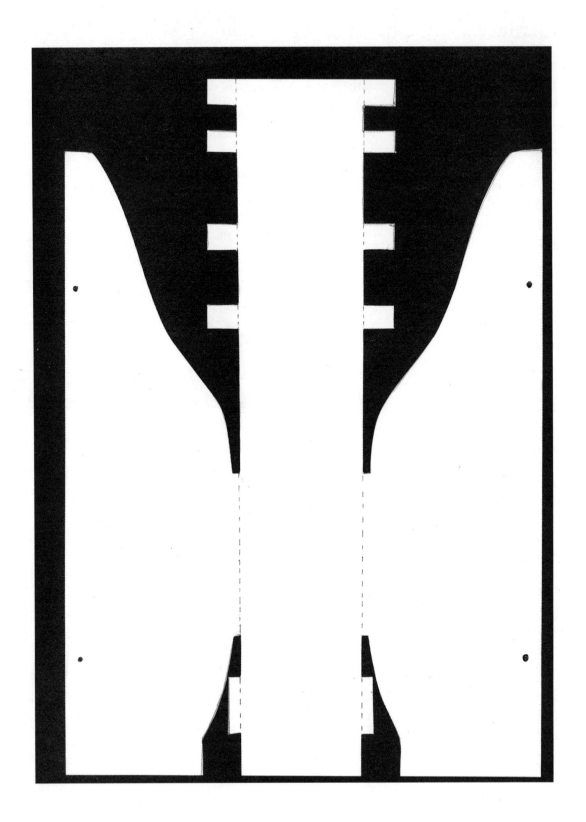

2. Carefully cut out the car. Discard the excess cardboard.

3. Using the metal ruler and the bone folder, score and fold along the dotted lines indicated on the template.

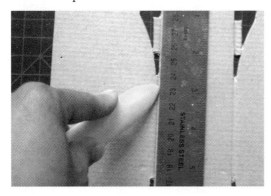

4. Carefully glue the tabs in place. This is the main body of the car.

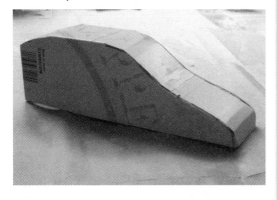

5. Using the awl, poke four holes in the main body of the car where indicated on the template. These will be where the wheels of the car attach.

6. Decorate the car with acrylic paints. Set aside and allow the paint to dry.

Adding wheels

7. Take a Ping-Pong ball and poke holes at the top and bottom with the awl.

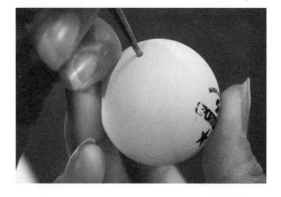

8. Unwind the **paper clip** to form a straight line.

9. Position the Ping-Pong ball inside the main body of the car so that the holes align with one set of wheel holes. Push the straightened paper clip through one wheel hole and add a

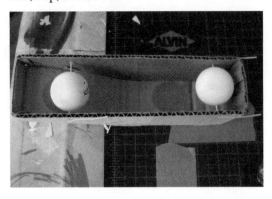

11. Repeat steps 7 through 10 with the remaining ball, clip, and beads.

bead before pushing through the Ping-Pong ball. Add a second bead before pushing through the other side of the main body of the car.

10. Using round-nose pliers, curl the exposed ends of the paper clip into a closed loop.

12. Cut two pieces of foil tape approximately 2 × ½ inches. Add to the front and back of the car.

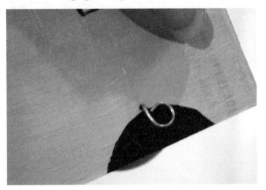

15. Picture Perfect Mobile

EVER WONDER what to do with all those school photos your children get every year? In addition to saving them for when your kids are old enough to regret certain style choices they adamantly made in their formative years, you can make this whimsical mobile.

The tools and techniques are largely borrowed from jewelry making, so expect a lot of bending and twisting of metal wires. Also, the sample below makes use of an incomplete deck of cards that seemed too nice to throw away.

Materials

7 school portraits, wallet size
7 playing cards or flash cards
"The mix"
11 large paper clips
1 wire from a used spiral notebook
1 piece butcher or thin cotton string, at least 2 feet long
1 roll transparent nylon string
7 small buttons

Tools

Waste sheets   1-inch paintbrush
Wire cutter   Brayer
Round-nose pliers   Craft knife
Chain-nose pliers   Metal ruler
⅛-inch hole puncher

Tip

• If you don't have any playing or flash cards, try using a food or a gift box.

Backing up the portraits

1. Match up one **portrait** to one **playing card,** using up all the photos and cards. With a brush, apply **"the mix"** to the card and place the photos on top.

2. Place a waste sheet on top of the photos. Take the brayer and roll over the waste sheet, ridding any air pockets between the photos and the cards. Carefully remove waste sheet.

3. With the craft knife and metal ruler, cut away any excess card or photo so that they are all the same size. Place the school portraits in between waste sheets and then place between two heavy books. Allow "the mix" to dry for at least an hour.

The mobile frame

4. Using a pair of chain-nose pliers, straighten the eleven **paper clips.**

5. Take four of the straightened paper clips and push a small button through each of them. Curl the paper clips at the end, using the round-nose pliers. Pinch the paper clips in the center so each one resembles an upside-down V. The button should sit at the apex of the upside-down V.

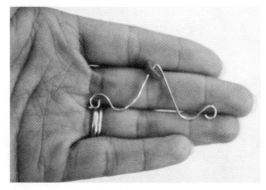

6. Curl the remaining seven paper clips at the end, using the round-nose pliers. Twist each of them around like a spring. Pull the top and bottom of each spring outward.

7. Attach one spring-shaped paper clip to the button at the pointed top of each V paper clip. Set them aside.

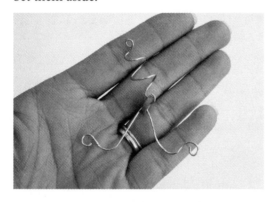

8. Straighten the **wire from a spiral notebook.** At the center, twist a small loop. This is the main frame. Attach a spring/V paper clip to the loop.

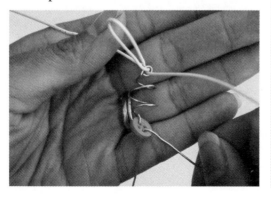

9. Attach another spring/V paper clip to one of the loops of the spring/V paper clip that is attached to the main frame. Then attach two spiral paper clips to the other loop.

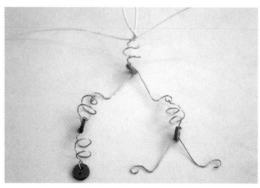

10. Slope down the ends of the main frame and twist each end into an open loop.

11. Twist the loops downward. Attach a spring/V paper clip to each open loop. Close up the loops.

12. Remove the school portraits from the heavy books and waste sheets. With a hole puncher, make holes centered at the top of each photo.

13. Double-knot pieces of **nylon string** at least 1 foot long to each photo.

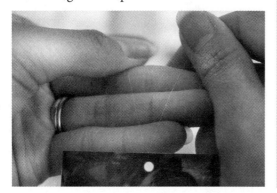

14. Tie **butcher string** to the main frame and hang it from the ceiling or a beam. Attach the photos to the main frame, varying the lengths to keep the mobile balanced.

16. Spare Parts Bear Doll

NOW THAT YOU'VE MADE at least three "sock" monkeys from chapter two (because you know that one "sock" monkey is clearly not enough), you should have leftover trunk pieces of girls' knitted tights. If you're feeling up to it, you can make a stuffed animal from these leftovers.

Because the body is made from two different trunk parts, this stuffed bear doll looks as if he is wearing a shirt and pants. For the face, try to use solid-color leftover pieces.

Materials

3 trunk pieces of girls' knitted tights
4 skeins of embroidery floss (2 of the same
    color + 1 black + 1 red)
1 old pillow (for stuffing)
Brown grocery bag

Tools

Scissors
Fine point black marker
Thick embroidery needle

Tip

- When selecting which leftovers to use, try to mix colors or patterns that complement each other.

The main body

1. **2 trunk pieces of knitted tights.** Trim down the two trunk pieces of knitted tights so they are approximately the same length. Sew up the leg holes of the tights. Set aside any leftover pieces. Choose one of the sewn trunk pieces to be the leg/lower abdomen and the other to be the arms/upper chest.

2. **Old pillow.** Take the leg/lower abdomen piece. Remove the stuffing from the pillow and add it to the legs/lower abdomen piece until it's filled out. Pull the arms trunk piece over the legs trunk piece until it reaches the waistline of the lower abdomen.

3. With a pair of sharp scissors, make a 2-inch incision in the crotch of the top trunk piece, between the arms where the neck should be. Add more stuffing to fill out the shoulder. Sew the two trunk pieces together at the waistline. This is the body of the bear.

4. At the neck opening, pull the legs trunk piece through until it's approximately 2 inches out. The opening should now resemble the top of a V-neck shirt with a turtleneck underneath. Sew the two trunk pieces together at the V-neck and the sides of the turtleneck.

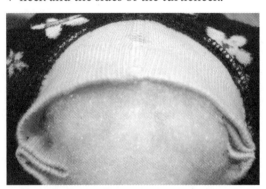

The head

5. **Brown grocery bag.** Draw a circle with a 7 inch diameter. At the bottom of the circle, add a rectangle that is 6 inches wide and 3 inches tall. Cut away excess from the bag and flip over. This is the head pattern.

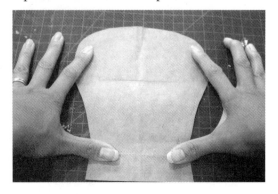

6. **Remaining trunk piece of knitted tights.** Take the head pattern and place it on top of the remaining "trunk" piece of knitted tights, around the buttocks area, waist-side down. With a fine point marker, lightly trace the pattern onto the tights.

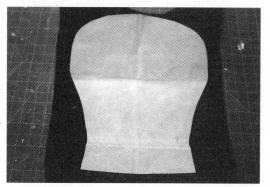

7. Cut out the head. Be sure to cut through two layers of the knitted tights so there are front and back pieces. Set aside any leftover pieces.

8. Sew the two pieces together, leaving the neck open. This is the head.

9. Stuff the head and sew the neck to the 2" incision in the main body. Before you finish sewing the head, add stuffing if the head, neck, or shoulders seem to droop.

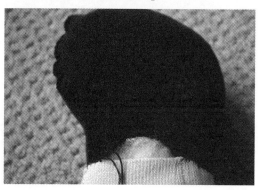

Finishing touches

10. Cut an oval measuring 5 inches across and 3 inches down from any leftover knitted pieces. This is the snout. Sew the snout to the center of the head, leaving a 1 inch hole. Stuff the snout and sew up the hole.

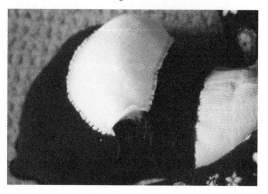

11. Sew a button to the middle of the snout. This is the nose.

12. Cut out two small triangles (no larger than 1½ inches long) from any leftover knitted pieces. Try to cut out front and back pieces. These are the ears. Sew an ear to each side of the head.

13. Cut out two small circles 1 inch in diameter from any leftover knitted pieces. Sew them to the head, above the snout. They should be evenly spaced.

14. With the black embroidery floss, stitch one button on top of each circle. These are the eyes.

15. With red embroidery floss, stitch a mouth below the nose on the snout.

17. Cherry Blossom Greeting Card

FOR A SCANT few weeks in April, the dominant color in Washington, D.C., is thankfully not red or blue, but pink. It comes from the cherry blossom trees that surround the grounds of the Washington Monument or the Tidal Basin in West Potomac Park and give this town a splash of pastel on an otherwise black and white facade.

Newspaper ads, with their matter-of-fact detail and neat columns, remind me of Washington's cool and distinct architecture. Juxtapose a tissue paper flower and voilà! You have a mini version of their famed cherry blossoms on a greeting card. It might even be too pretty to give away or inspire you to make more than just one.

Materials

1 brown paper grocery bag
1 white cardboard (from T-shirt or bedding packaging)
Newspaper want ads
Pink tissue paper
Craft glue stick

Tools

Bone folder
Scissors
Paper cutter
Toothpick

Dry paintbrush
Black fine-point permanent marker

Tip

- If you want to add a little bit more dimension and color to the cherry blossoms, cut out additional smaller almond shapes in a lighter colored tissue paper. Add them on top of the first layer of cherry blossom leaves in step 13.

Base card

1. Fold the **cardboard** in half lengthwise. Using the paper cutter, trim down the folded cardboard to 4¼ × 5½ inches. This is your base card.

2. Apply a thin layer of glue to the front panel. Place the newspaper on top and smooth out any air pockets with the bone folder.

3. Turn over the card so the newspaper is on the bottom. Carefully trim off any excess newspaper away from the edges of the folded base card.

The tree

4. Place the folded base card on top of the **brown paper grocery bag.** With a pencil, lightly trace the outer perimeter of the card on the grocery bag.

5. Remove the folded base card. Inside the rectangle, lightly draw the trunk and branches of a tree.

6. Place the grocery bag on top of the cutting mat. With the craft knife, cut out the tree.

7. Place the tree on top of the front panel of the folded base card. The tree should extend slightly past the borders of the base card. Glue the tree in place.

8. Smooth out any excess air pockets between the tree and the surface of the front panel with the bone folder.

9. Trim off any excess pieces of the tree.

The cherry blossoms

10. Fold the **tissue paper** in half at least three times. With the craft knife, cut out small almond shapes ¼ to ½ inch in length.

11. Repeat step 10 several times so that you have at least thirty-six pieces. These will become the leaves of the cherry blossoms.

12. Using the toothpick, apply small amounts of glue from a glue stick to either the individual leaf or the front panel of the card. Arrange the petals, four to one cherry blossom, around the branches of the tree.

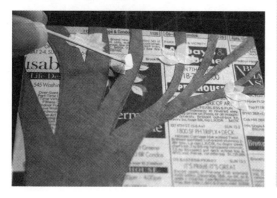

13. With a dry paintbrush, sweep the surface of the front panel, using short strokes.

14. Add the words "Spring Has Arrived!" to the front panel, using a black fine-point permanent marker.

May

Projects This Month

Colorful Garden Butterflies

Paper Flowers

Paper Lantern

Don't Forget Your Mother's Day Card

Handy Handbag

APRIL SHOWERS bring May flowers, right?

Well, in addition to flowers, May brings in other unspecified plants, butterflies, pesky insects, Cinco de Mayo, Mother's Day, and the unveiling of the much beloved outdoor grill. Most of us are really getting out of the house by now, eating our meals at picnic tables, reading the newspaper under a shady tree, or running around just to feel the warmth of the sun on our skin.

I get ambitious in May, planning out the forthcoming summer's dinner parties which would hopefully make use of our backyard. So I begin to decorate. This month's crafts are all things we can use in and around the yard—except the Mother's Day card, of course. I threw that one in because you should never forget about Mom (right, Mom?)—ever! (Right, kids?)

Materials you will need this month

1 magazine sheet

1 business card

White permanent glue

1 bamboo skewer, 12 inches long

12 pieces decorative tissue paper, any color

1 glass Coke bottle or salad dressing bottle

string, 9 feet long

4 brown paper grocery bags

One string Christmas lights

1 thick sheet white paper

1 photocopy of a picture of Mom in her heyday, made on thick copy paper

1 cereal box

1 piece thin cotton fabric, approximately 5 × 6 inches
1 small button
2 skeins embroidery floss
2 items of clothing large enough to yield two 10 × 24-inch pieces fabric
Regular cotton thread
1 zipper, 12 inches long

May holidays, typical and not-so

Lumpy Rug Day (3rd)

Cinco de Mayo (5th)

National Teacher's Day (1st Tuesday of the first full week)

No Socks Day (8th)

Lost Sock Memorial Day (9th)

Clean Up Your Room Day (10th)

Limerick Day (12th)

Tulip Day (13th)

National Dance like a Chicken Day (14th)

Mother's Day (2nd Sunday)

National Chocolate Chip Day (15th)

International Museum Day (18th)

National Waitresses/Waiters Day (21st)

National Tap Dance Day (25th)

National Hamburger Day (28th)

Memorial Day (last Monday)

National Macaroon Day (31st)

Monthlong celebrations

Asian Pacific American Heritage Month

Asthma and Allergy Awareness Month

American Bike Month

Better Sleep Month

Mental Health Month

National Good Car Care Month

National Photo Month

National Salad Month

National Egg Month

National Barbecue Month

Revise Your Work Schedule Month

National Physical Fitness and Sports Month

National Hamburger Month

Fungal Infection Awareness

May birthdays of famous people

Dr. Benjamin Spock (2nd)

Audrey Hepburn (4th)

Sigmund Freud (6th)

Robert Browning (7th)

Harry S. Truman (8th)

Martha Graham (11th)

Irving Berlin (11th)

Florence Nightingale (12th)

Jasper Johns (15th)

Malcolm X (19th)

Jimmy Stewart (20th)

Mary Cassatt (22nd)

Bob Dylan (24th)

Ralph W. Emerson (25th)

Dashiell Hammett (27th)

Wild Bill Hickok (27th)

John F. Kennedy (29th)

Bob Hope (29th)

Patrick Henry (29th)

Walt Whitman (31st)

18. Colorful Garden Butterflies

My kids love butterflies. Ever since we went to the Bronx Zoo's Butterfly House, they've wanted butterflies flying around the backyard. Although we get our share of butterflies during the warmer months, it's never enough. Only an unnatural onslaught of these colorful winged insects would satisfy my kids (and scare any sane human being). Using a simple tea bag–folding technique and some magazines, my kids and I make these butterflies to decorate our garden. To keep them lasting a bit longer, we usually remove them before it rains.

Materials

> 1 magazine sheet
> 1 business card
> White permanent glue
> 1 bamboo skewer, 12 inches long

Tools

> Paper cutter
> Pencil
> Craft knife

Tip

- Choose magazine ads or covers that have a bit of glossy varnish or lamination to them. Not only are they more colorful, the varnish or lamination will make the butterflies more resistant to dirt and wind.

The wings

1. Cut out two 5-inch squares from the **magazine sheet.**

2. Take one of the squares and fold in half along the diagonal to form a triangle.

3. Turn the triangle so that the long side is vertical and the pointed end faces left. Fold horizontally in half and unfold.

4. Pull up the pointed end from left to right, past the long vertical side by about ½ inch. Fold it down.

5. Locate the two points where the folded down pointed end meets the long vertical side.

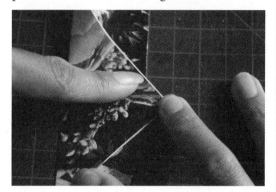

6. Fold the top and bottom portions, starting your fold at the left middle crease made in step 3. The outer edges should touch the two points in step 5. This is one butterfly wing.

7. Repeat steps 2 through 6 for the second butterfly wing.

The body

8. Choose which side of the **business card** you want shown. Have that side face down. Fold the card in half lengthwise.

9. Place one of the wings on top of the folded business card so the pointed end nearly touches the middle crease of the business card. There should be ⅛ inch between the pointed end of the wing and the middle crease of the business card. Lightly trace the outline of the wing.

10. Remove the wing. Draw the profile of a butterfly body, head, and antennae.

11. Cut away excess pieces from the folded business card. Unfold the card. This is the butterfly body.

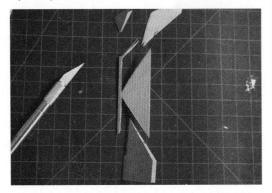

12. Glue the wings on to the body.

13. Fold the body in the other direction.

14. Glue the **skewer** to the inside fold of the body. Be sure the pointy end of the skewer is at the bottom.

19. Paper Flowers

OH, YES, there are many reasons to make paper flowers this month. These paper roses are a quick Mother's Day bouquet that doesn't require much maintenance, or a May Day craft that you can do with your kids. Regardless of how nimble your hands may or may not be, it's pretty hard to not make an attractive rose.

And for husbands out there who have forgotten their wedding anniversary—and you know who you are—I've seen roses made out of paper napkins and toilet tissue. This means that you have absolutely no excuse for not bringing home flowers. Just don't use the dirty ones. Yeeeuck!

Materials

12 pieces of decorative tissue paper, any color
1 glass Coke bottle or salad dressing bottle
1 piece string, at least 6 inches long
1 brown paper grocery bag

Tools

Scissors
Green permanent marker or watercolor paint

Tip

• Don't be afraid of using tissue paper that has any sort of graphics printed on it (store logo, words, and so on). They can add a bit of flavor to roses that have plain solid colors if you mix them together in the same vase.

Making a rose

1. Cut a piece of **tissue paper** to 12 × 8 inches.

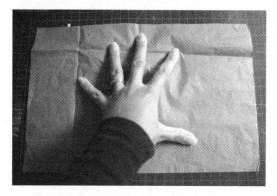

2. Make a horizontal fold, leaving 1 inch of space at the bottom.

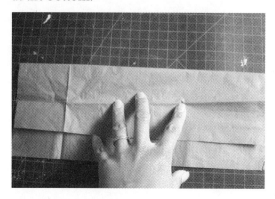

3. Crinkle the paper slightly to give it more volume.

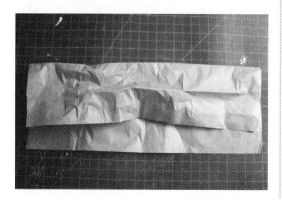

4. Holding the folded edge with the tips of your fingers, loosely roll the tissue paper around your fingers.

5. Twist the bottom. This is the rose.

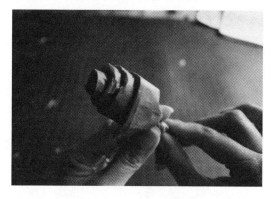

6. Gently pull the middle of the rose up to get a more rounded look.

7. Repeat steps 1 through 5 until you have twelve roses.

8. Arrange the roses into a bouquet and tie them together.

Making leaves

9. From the **brown paper grocery bag** cut eight long strips measuring 8 × 1 inches.

10. Bevel the edges of each strip on one side.

11. With a green marker or watercolor paint, color the strips of bag.

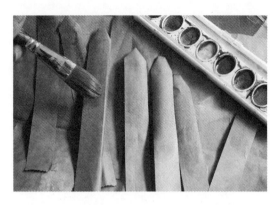

12. Twist the end of the strip that is not beveled until you have a 4-inch stem. These are the leaves.

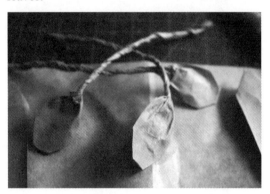

Putting it all together

13. Place the flowers in the **glass Coke bottle.**

14. Stick the leaves in the bouquet.

20. Paper Lantern

EVER WONDERED what to do with those Christmas lights during the rest of the year? Or maybe you bought one of those fake trees that already come with lights and don't know whether you should throw out the old ones? Well, here's a bright (excuse the horrible pun) idea.

Make a festive paper lantern for all those outdoor dinner parties you'll be throwing.

Materials

1 thick sheet white copy paper
3 large brown paper grocery bags
Craft glue stick
One string Christmas lights
String, at least 8 feet

Tools

Scissors
Craft knife
Paper clips

Tip

• Practice making your own pattern on 10-inch-square sheets that you fold down to 5 inches square and then fold once more along the diagonal (see steps 4 and 5). Once you design a pattern that you like, photocopy your folded pattern and then follow the instructions from steps 6 to 14.

The lantern

1. Photocopy this pattern onto a **thick sheet of white paper** *at 300 percent.*

2. Using the craft knife, cut out the pattern and discard any excess paper.

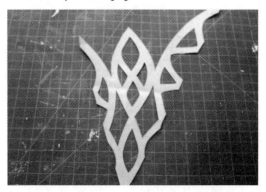

3. Take **3 brown paper grocery bags** apart at the seams. Flatten them out on your worktable.

4. Fold the bags into quarters.

5. Fold the bags one more time on the diagonal. (Be sure that one point of the diagonal is at the center of the bag when unfolded.)

6. Place the pattern over one bag. Trace the pattern with a pencil. Repeat on the other two folded bags.

7. Using the scissors, cut out the overall shape made by the pattern as well as larger parts of the design.

8. Using the craft knife, cut out the more intricate elements of the design.

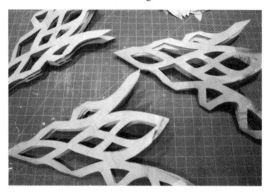

9. Unfold the bags to reveal three large paper flowers. Set one of them aside. Place the remaining two on top of each other so that they match. On one half of the flower glue together at the outer edges.

10. Lift the top paper flower. Take the third paper flower and glue it at the edges on one side, leaving an opening on the opposite side.

The inside lights

11. Take the end of the **string of Christmas lights** and tie into a loose ball approximately 3 inches in diameter.

12. Place the ball end of the string inside the paper flower. Glue the remaining outer edges of the paper flower so that the ball is securely inside.

13. Hang the lights from the ceiling or a beam. Determine how high you would like the paper lantern to hang.

Putting it all together

14. Secure a piece of **string** from the very top of the paper lantern to the ceiling so that it is holding it up. It should not be dependent on the string of lights to stay up.

21. Don't Forget Your Mother's Day Card

I'm a mother. I have a mother. I also have two sisters, a mother-in-law, and several friends who have the (mostly) good fortune of being someone's mom. And you know what? We all like to celebrate this day and it doesn't take much to make us happy. We're not asking for a lot—a card will do just fine.

Oh, sure, you can buy a card that says what you feel, but why don't you write what you feel in a card made by you?

Materials

1 photocopy of a picture of Mom in her
    heyday, made on thick copy paper
Craft glue stick
1 cereal box
1 piece thin cotton fabric, approximately 5 × 6
    inches
1 small button
1 skein embroidery floss

Tools

Paper cutter	4 binder clips or
Metal ruler	clothespins
Bone folder	Beeswax
Craft knife	Thick embroidery
Pencil	needle
Awl	

Tip

• Size of picture should be able to fit into a 1½ × 2½-inch rectangular frame. Make a sample frame out of any piece of paper to help select the appropriate photograph. You can reduce the size of your picture to accommodate the frame by copying the photograph at a smaller percentage, which might take a few tries.

Base card

1. Using the paper cutter, cut down the **cereal box** to a rectangle measuring 8¼ × 5½ inches. Mark the vertical center of the rectangle at 4⅛ inches. Using the bone folder and metal ruler, score the cardboard and fold in half. This is your base card.

2. Unfold the base card so that the back and front panels face up. In the center of the front panel, measure and cut out a rectangle measuring 1½ × 2½ inches. This is the picture frame.

3. On the front panel, lightly draw a rectangular border ½ inch from the edge of the picture frame. With the awl, punch out small holes along the border about ½ inch apart. Be sure to start at one corner of the border.

Adding the detail

4. Apply a thin later of glue to the front panel. Place the **cotton fabric** over the front panel and gently smooth out any air pockets with the bone folder. Flip the base card over so that the inside front and back panels are facing up. Cut off the excess fabric at a 45-degree angle on the two outer corners.

5. Apply glue to three edges of the inside front panel. Pull fabric over the edges and smooth out air pockets with the bone folder. You may

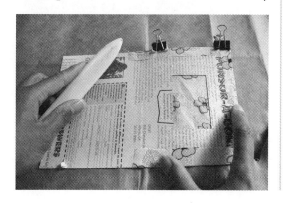

need to use binder clips or clothespins to hold the fabric down while the glue dries.

6. Inside the picture frame, cut diagonal slits into the exposed cotton fabric from each corner. Be sure that the slits intersect with each other.

7. Apply glue to the edges of the frame and pull fabric on all four sides inside the picture frame. Again, you may need to use binder clips or clothespins to hold the fabric down while the glue dries.

8. Once the glue is dry, fold the base card so that the back panel is facing up. With the metal ruler and craft knife, remove any excess fabric from the folded edge of the card. Add a little bit of glue to the edges of the fabric to prevent it from fraying.

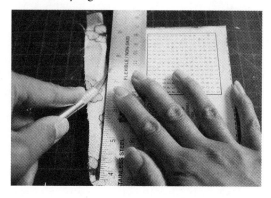

9. Wax a piece of **embroidery floss** about the length of your outstretched arms. Thread your needle with the floss and, starting from the in-

side front panel, stitch the border created in step 5.

10. Add glue to the edges of the **photo** and place it on the inside front panel within the picture frame.

The closure

11. Unfold the card so that the back and front panels are facing up. On the right edge of the front panel, cut out a sideways V-shaped notch in the center. The open end of the V should not measure more than ½ inch and the distance from the right edge should be approximately ¼ inch.

12. Fold the card so the front panel is facing up. Place the small **button** on top of the V notch. Using the awl, punch holes through the button holes and into the back panel.

13. Unfold the card so the inside front and back panels are facing up. Using the holes made in step 13, sew the button to the inside back panel.

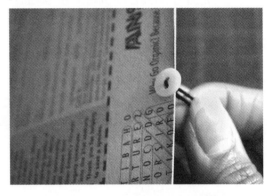

14. When you are done, you should be able to slide the V notch in the front panel underneath the button.

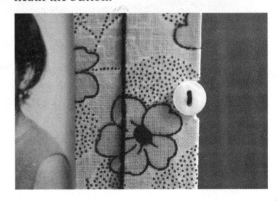

22. Handy Handbag

EVER LOOK at a skirt or a blouse and think to your-self, "Boy, wouldn't that make a really nice bag"?

After finally coming to the realization that certain fashion trends really aren't making a come-back, I decided to live out this fantasy of making a bag out of clothing. I think that mixing fabrics and patterns really make this simple handbag more lux-urious than it is. And it can stylishly turn into a lunch bag for dining al fresco on a sunny day.

Materials

2 items of clothing large enough to yield two
　　10 × 24-inch pieces fabric
Thread
Embroidery floss
1 zipper, 12 inches long

Tools

Long ruler　　　　Embroidery needle
Scissors　　　　　Iron
Thick sewing needle

Tips

• If you don't have items of clothing large enough to yield two 10 × 24-inch pieces, four 10 × 12-inch will do. Simply sew the pieces together to get two 10 × 24-inch pieces.

• If you want to make a shoulder bag instead, dou-ble the measurements for the fabric and the zipper.

The bag

1. Cut down the **clothing** to two 10 × 24-inch pieces of fabric. Set aside any leftover mate-rial.

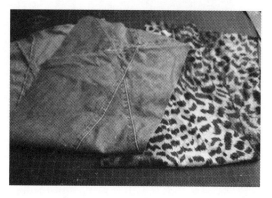

2. Fold one piece of fabric in half to measure 10 × 12 inches. Sew up the left and right sides with regular thread and the sewing needle, leaving an opening on the top.

3. Repeat step 2 on the second 10 × 24-inch piece of fabric.

4. Turn one of the sewn pieces inside out so that the stitches are inside.

5. Place the second sewn piece inside the one that is inside out. This is the bag.

6. Sew the tops together, using **embroidery floss** and the embroidery needle.

7. Fold the top down to form a 2-inch cuff. Use the iron to press the crease of the cuff. Unfold the cuff.

Attaching the straps and zipper

8. From the leftover material, cut out four 24 × 2-inch strips.

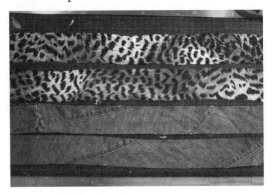

9. Sew the strips together to make two straps. 24 × 1 inches.

10. Sew the straps to the side of the bag. Be sure the stitches and at least 1 inch of each end of the strap are below the crease in the cuff.

11. Sew the **zipper** inside the opening of the bag. The stitches should be below the crease of the cuff.

The final touches

12. Fold the cuff down. At one side of the cuff, sew it to the seam of the side of the bag. Repeat on the other side.

13. Flatten the bottom of the bag so the corners are pointed out. Pull the corners 1 inch up the sides and sew to the seam.

14. Use the iron on the finished bag to tighten folds and creases.

June

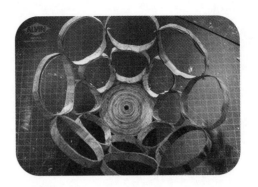

Projects This Month

Map Basket
Sack Full o' Sand Toys
Father's Day Card
Sun Hat

SUMMER IS FINALLY HERE. If you're like me, then you try to go to the beach as much as humanly possible. And if you're really like me (oh, please say you are!) then you pack your beach bags the day before and leave them by the front door—despite not having beach plans for a few days. Nothing says summer more than a calendar filled with vacation days spent away from home. That is, unless you are lucky enough to live by the beach. (And can I be your best friend?)

This month we will make things that get a lot of use. Hopefully, you will head to the beach and use the sand toys with your kids, protect that precious head of yours (or your children) with the sun hat, and not forget to make a card for dear ole dad. And those maps you saved from that recent road trip to the beach? Well, how's about making a pretty cool basket?

Materials you will need this month

2 maps
Linen thread
1 gallon milk or juice container
1 half-gallon plastic milk or juice container
1 half-gallon milk or juice carton
1 round plastic container (from butter or cream cheese)
1 produce net bag
Thin nylon rope, 2 feet
1 store gift box, top and bottom
1 photograph
Yarn or thin ribbon
2 canvas tote bags
Black piping, 3 feet

Thread

1 brown paper grocery bag

June holidays, typical and not-so

Dare Day (1st)

National Rocky Road Ice Cream Day (2nd)

Repeat Day (3rd) (Repeat Day . . . .)

Festival Of Popular Delusions Day (5th)

National Doughnut Day (1st Friday)

National Gingerbread Day (6th)

National Chocolate Ice Cream Day (7th)

Name Your Poison Day (8th)

Donald Duck Day (9th)

National Yo-Yo Day (10th)

National Hug Holiday (11th)

National Juggling Day (13th)

Flag Day (14th)

Smile Power Day (15th)

National Hollerin' Contest Day (16th)

Father's Day (3rd Sunday)

International Panic Day (18th)

Ice Cream Soda Day (20th)

National Chocolate Eclair Day (22nd)

National Chocolate Pudding Day (26th)

Paul Bunyan Day (28th)

Meteor Day (30th)

Monthlong celebrations

Adopt-a-Shelter-Cat Month

American Rivers Month

Cancer in the Sun Month

Dairy Month

Gay Pride Month

Turkey Lover's Month

National Accordion Awareness Month

National Fresh Fruit and Vegetable Month

National Ice Tea Month

National Papaya Month

National Pest Control Month

National Rose Month

Fight the Filthy Fly Month

Zoo and Aquarium Month

June birthdays of famous people

Marilyn Monroe (1st)

Hedda Hopper (2nd)

Josephine Baker (3rd)

Frank Lloyd Wright (8th)

Cole Porter (9th)

Maurice Sendak (10th)

Judy Garland (10th)

Vince Lombardi (11th)

Jacques Cousteau (11th)

Anne Frank (12th)

George H. W. Bush (12th)

William Butler Yeats (13th)

Harriet Beecher Stowe (14th)

Waylon Jennings (15th)

Lou Gehrig (19th)

Al Hirschfeld (21st)

Billy Wilder (22nd)

Pearl S. Buck (26th)

Bob "Captain Kangaroo" Keeshan (27th)

Helen Keller (27th)

23. Map Basket

No, it's not a basket to hold your maps. It's a basket *made* of maps. How many times have you been on vacation and saved each and every map? Museum, public transportation, and driving maps are the usual suspects. The more interesting maps I've saved are of a brewery, a potato chip factory, and a book catalog. And I usually save more than one of every map.

Hmm, maybe I do need a basket to hold my maps. But this map basket is as incredibly useful as it is pretty.

Materials

2 maps
Linen thread
White permanent glue

Tools

Paper cutter   Awl
Long metal ruler   Thick sewing needle
Bone folder   Pencil
Paper clips

Tip

• Try experimenting with one of the folded strips for other designs. Be sure you are able to repeat it on the other seven strips and can sew them together easily.

The main basket

1. With the paper cutter, cut sixteen 2-inch strips from the two maps. Set aside eight of them for the bottom piece.

2. Place the long metal ruler along one strip. Score and fold strip in half so that it is 1 inch wide.

3. Score and fold again so that strip is ½ inch wide. Repeat step on the remaining seven strips.

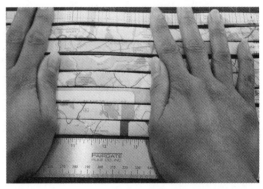

4. Take one of the folded strips and form a figure eight. Glue the ends and hold in place with paper clips. Allow time for glue to dry.

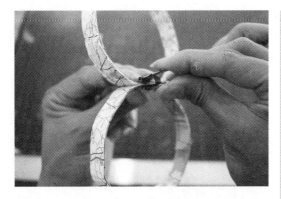

5. Repeat step 4 on the remaining seven folded strips.

6. Using the awl, poke eight holes into every folded strip, at the location indicated in the picture above.

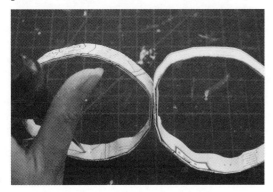

7. Sew the strips together with the **linen thread.** Make an individual stitch for each set of holes.

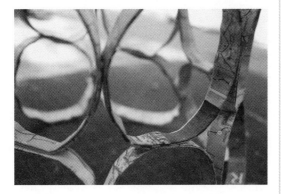

The basket bottom

8. Take the remaining eight strips and fold each one down to ½ inch wide.

9. Take one folded strip and add a thin line of glue to one side.

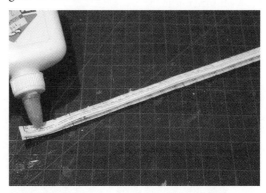

10. Wrap it around a pencil to form a disk.

11. Add two more folded strips to the disk by adding a thin line of glue to one side and wrapping it around. This is the basket bottom.

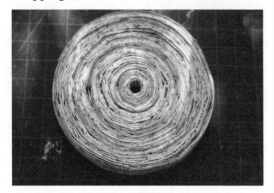

12. Take the main basket and poke two holes that are ½ inch apart at the bottom circle of every figure eight.

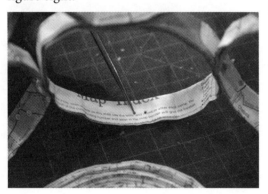

13. Poke 16 holes on the outer edges of the basket bottom that would correspond to the holes of the main basket.

14. Sew the main basket and the bottom together.

24. Sack Full o' Sand Toys

How many times have you had to replace yet another beach shovel and pail, knowing that it was only a matter of time before you would need to do it all over again? My son is notorious for losing his sand toys. He once believed that burying them in the sand would prevent them from being stolen and he would not need to collect them at the end of the day. The only problem with this bit of lazy thinking was that there was no way to make a permanent marker in the sand and therefore know exactly where the toys are buried.

So I've become accustomed to fashioning sand toys out of our recyclables. It saves me a trip to the toy store—as well as a couple of bucks.

Materials
1 gallon milk or juice container
1 half-gallon plastic milk or juice container

1 half-gallon milk or juice carton
1 round plastic container (from butter or
   cream cheese)
1 produce net bag
Thin nylon rope, 2 feet

Tools

Ruler	Craft knife
Fine-point	Sandpaper
permanent marker	

Tip

- If the containers are plain looking, it might be best not to try to color them. After a few days in the sand, the surface will be scratched and any kind of design you put on it may be just a waste of time.

The large shovel

1. Be sure to keep the cap on the top of the **gallon milk container** screwed on tightly. Place the container right side up on your worktable, with the handle on the left side. With the fine-point marker draw a diagonal line down from the bottom of the handle to the right corner.

2. Turn container around so the handle is on the right side. Draw a diagonal line down from the bottom of the handle to the left corner.

3. Turn the container around so the handle is at the back. Draw a line connecting the two lines at the bottom edge of the container.

4. Using a craft knife, carefully cut out the bottom of the container, using the lines as guides. This is your large shovel.

The small shovel

5. Repeat steps 1 through 4 on the **half-gallon plastic container.** This is your small shovel.

The square brick mold

6. Place the **half-gallon carton** right side up on your worktable. Measure 5 inches from the bottom on all four corners and draw a horizontal line around the carton.

7. Using the craft knife and metal ruler, cut off the top of the carton at the 5-inch horizontal line. This is your square brick mold.

The round brick mold

8. If the round plastic container is taller than 6 inches, you might want to cut it down.

Otherwise, you do not have to do anything further.

9. If you do need to cut down the container, measure 5 inches from the bottom and draw a horizontal line all around the sides. Using the craft knife, cut off the excess part of the container. This is the round brick mold.

Putting it all together

10. Remove any tags from the **net bag.** With the scissors, cut the top of the bag so that it has an even edge.

11. Weave the **rope** along the top of the bag. Pull it so there is a 5-inch tail on either end.

12. Tie the ends into a knot.

13. With the sandpaper, sand down the edges of the toys.

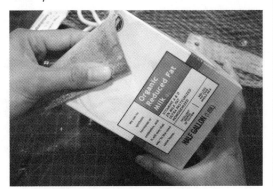

14. Place toys in the bag.

25. Father's Day Card

WELL, LAST MONTH we gave Mom her due. Now it's Dad's turn. This simple pop-up card has a great closure that ensures the surprise will be well kept within the panels of the card. In the sample below, I used a picture of my son in his early years. It's a photo that is very nostalgic for my father who seems, in retirement, more ready than ever to play with his grandchildren.

Happy Father's Day, Dad.

Materials

1 store gift box, top and bottom
1 photograph
Craft glue stick
Yarn or thin ribbon

Tools

Paper cutter	Pencil
Metal ruler	Awl
Craft knife	Embroidery needle or
Bone folder	thick sewing needle

Tip

- Store gift boxes may be a thing of the past now that everyone is being eco-conscious. You can use any plain thin card from any of your recyclables as long as it's large enough.

Base card

1. Using the paper cutter, cut from the **gift box** a piece of flat cardboard measuring 9⅜ × 5½ inches.

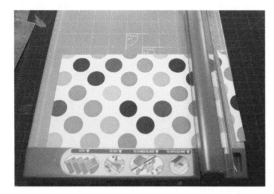

2. Turn the cardboard into the landscape position (the 9⅜-inch width at the bottom). Measure and score a vertical line at 3⅜ inches from the left edge. Then measure and score a vertical line 1 inch from the right edge.

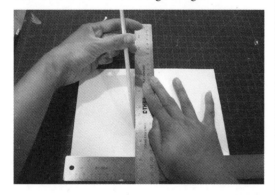

3. Fold and unfold the cardboard along the two vertical lines. This is your base card.

The pop-up

4. Cut a piece of cardboard measuring 6 × 5½ inches. Place on your worktable so that the 6-inch side is horizontal. Measure and score a vertical line 3⅜ inches from the left edge.

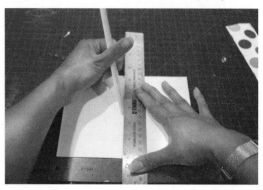

5. Fold along the vertical line. Turn cardboard 90 degrees clockwise so the folded edge is at the bottom. Measure 1 inch from the left and right edges and mark with the pencil.

6. At the 1-inch marks, make a ¾-inch incision. With the bone folder and metal ruler, score a

horizontal line connecting the tops of the incision. Flip the folded cardboard over and repeat. Unfold the cardboard and push the middle up. This is the pop-up.

7. Cut out a rectangular piece of cardboard measuring 3½ × 3 inches. Cut out an inner rectangle approximately ¼ inch from the outer edge. This is your picture frame.

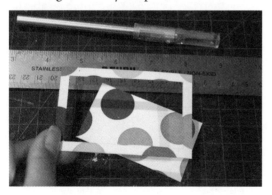

8. Place the picture frame on top of your **photograph.** Trim off the excess parts of the photo so it fits inside the frame.

9. Add glue to the edges of the photo and place the frame on top. Flip over and add glue to the bottom portion of the photo/frame. Place on the bottom part of the pop-up and close.

10. Add glue to one side of the folded pop-up and place inside the base card. Be sure it fits snugly in the crease of the card.

11. Add glue to the other side of pop-up and close the base card. Press down firmly for a few seconds and then allow a few minutes for the glue to dry.

The closure

12. Fold the scored vertical line 1 inch from the right edge. Lightly draw a vertical line ½ inch from the folded right edge. With the awl, poke a hole along this vertical line that centered from the top and bottom.

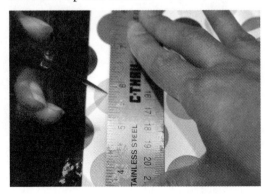

13. Along this same vertical line, poke two holes above the center hole, 1 inch apart. Then poke two holes below the center hole, 1 inch apart. You should have a total of five equidistant holes.

14. Starting from the middle hole and using either thin ribbon or yarn, make a pamphlet stitch (see page 5). You should be able to insert the front panel of the card inside the cuff.

26. Sun Hat

EVERY YEAR I attend a conference and walk away with a bunch of canvas tote bags. I use them when I go grocery shopping, shlep a towel to the pool, or transport food to a party. There isn't a canvas tote bag in my house that has not gotten its share of use. But every so often, I realize that I have too many. So I turn them into other well-used items, such as this sun hat.

Materials

1 brown paper grocery bag
2 canvas tote bags
Black piping, 3 feet
Thread

Tools

Ruler   Scissors
Compass   Needle
Pencil

Tip

- Try to use thinner canvas bags, which are easier to cut and sew.

Making the pattern

1. Draw the following pieces on the **brown paper grocery bag:**
   - Circle 6½ inches in diameter

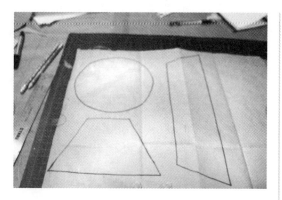

- Trapezoid that measures 9¾ inches at the top, 11¾ inches at the bottom, and 3½ inches on the sides
- Trapezoid that measures 3 inches at the top, 5¼ inches at the bottom, and 4½ inches on the sides.

2. Cut out the three shapes and label them as follows:
   - Circle: top
   - Large trapezoid: side
   - Small trapezoid: edge

Cutting and sewing

3. Take one **canvas tote bag** and cut out the following:
   - 1 top
   - 2 sides
   - 8 edges

4. Place the sides on top of each other so they match. Use the **thread** to sew the sides together at the left and right edges.

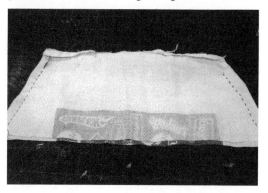

5. There are two openings: one smaller one at the top, and one larger one at the bottom. The smaller opening should have a circumference that measures approximately 19 inches (give or take ⅛ inch). Sew on the top, making sure that the stitches are on the same side as the ones in the sides.

6. Sew the edges together at the side, making sure that you keep all the tops together and the bottoms together.

7. There are two openings: one smaller one at the top, and one larger one at the bottom. The smaller opening should have a circumference that measures approximately 23 inches (give or take ¼ inch). Sew on the sides, making sure that the stitches are on the same side.

8. Repeat steps 3 through 7 on the second canvas tote bag.

Putting it all together

9. You should now have two sewn pieces of the hat. Determine which one is the lining and the outside.

10. Take the outside piece and turn it inside out so that the stitches are on the underside.

11. Place the outside piece on top of the lining and try to align the edges as much as possible.

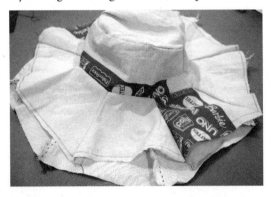

12. Sew the bottoms of the edges together.

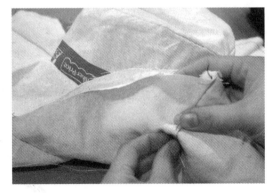

13. Turn the entire hat inside out to expose the lining. If the hat is not holding its shape well, place a couple of discreet stitches along the sides so that the outside and the lining stay together.

14. Turn hat right side out and sew black piping to the edges.

July

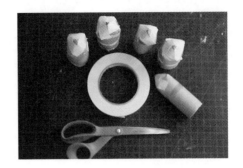

Projects This Month

Outdoor Serving Bowls

Sun Piñata

Pinwheel

Toy Dump Truck

SUMMER IS IN FULL SWING and you haven't eaten indoors for weeks. And why should you? July is the perfect outdoor food month, with monthlong celebratory observations of various picnic foods and holidays that tell you to eat up. July is certainly my kind of month. I often dream of eating for sport, such as the Nathan's Hot Dog Eating Contest at Coney Island in New York.

So who's with me? Eat your heart out, Takeru Kobayashi (six-time winner of the Annual Nathan's Hot Dog Eating Contest). And I'm talking to you, Joey Chestnut of San Jose (2007 and 2008 winner). You're going down!

Materials you will need this month

1 brown paper grocery bag

Large balloon

Newspaper

5 empty toilet paper rolls

1 empty paper towel roll

Yellow tempera paint

Yellow tissue paper

Black, orange, and gold acrylic paint

Lots o' candy

String

8 magazine sheets

Yellow duct tape, 3 inches wide

Black electrical tape, 1 inch wide

Metallic tape, 3 inches wide

1 chopstick or wooden paint mixing stick

1 paper clip

1 button
1 bead
1 small round plastic lid (from a sour cream or butter container)
1 half-gallon milk or juice carton
1 round plastic 16-ounce container
4 vitamin bottle caps
6 paper clips
4 buttons or beads

July holidays, typical and not-so

Stay out of the Sun Day (3rd)
Independence Day (4th)
National Fried Chicken Day (6th)
National Strawberry Sundae Day (7th)
National Sugar Cookie Day (9th)
National Cheer Up the Lonely Day (11th)
National Pecan Pie Day (12th)
National Nude Day (14th)
National Tapioca Pudding Day (15th)
National Peach Ice Cream Day (17th)
Ugly Truck Contest Day (20th)
National Tug-of-War Tournament Day (21st)
National Ice Cream Day (3rd Sunday)
National Hot Dog Day (23rd)
Amelia Earhart Day (24th)
Aunt and Uncle Day (26th)
Take Your Pants for a Walk Day (27th)
National Milk Chocolate Day (28th)
National Cheesecake Day (30th)

Monthlong celebrations

National Baked Beans Month
National Blueberry Month
National Ice Cream Month
National Hot Dog Month
National Tennis Month
"Read an Almanac" Month
and Anti-Boredom Month

July birthdays of famous people

Thurgood Marshall (2nd)
George M. Cohan (3rd)
Calvin Coolidge (4th)
P. T. Barnum (5th)
Dalai Lama (6th)
John Paul Jones (6th)
Nelson Rockefeller (8th)
John D. Rockefeller (8th)
E. B. White (11th)
John Quincy Adams (11th)
George Washington Carver (12th)
Henry David Thoreau (12th)
Gerald R. Ford (14th)
James Cagney (17th)
Nelson Mandela (18th)
Ernest Hemingway (21st)
Alexander Calder (22nd)
Amelia Earhart (24th)
Stanley Kubrick (26th)
Jacqueline Kennedy Onassis (28th)
Stanley Kunitz (29th)
Henry Ford (30th)

27. Outdoor Serving Bowls

WHENEVER MY KIDS have their friends over for some backyard fun, I like to serve chips and popcorn in these serving bowls. In the past, I've used plastic bowls, but even plastic can shatter—especially when hurled by a young child at speeds that defy logic.

So make a few of these bowls and keep them around during the summer months. To get more use out of them, line them with a paper towel before adding those salty snacks and wipe clean after every use. But be sure to never use anything remotely resembling a liquid in these bowls. They are, after all, made of papier-mâché.

Materials

Food coloring
1 brown paper grocery bag, crumpled into a ball
Papier-mâché paste (see page xvii)
Newspaper

Tools

A mixing bowl or   ½-inch pastry
  plastic container   paintbrush
2 glass or ceramic   Clear plastic wrap
  serving bowls of
  equal size

Tip

• Since working with papier-mâché is quite messy, it might make sense to make more than one bowl at a time. Smaller bowls are great for sending kids outside with snacks. Just be sure they don't leave the bowls outside overnight, lest you want to wake up to soggy mounds of paper scattered all over your yard.

The bowl

1. In the mixing bowl mix a few drops of food coloring with ½ cup of water.

2. Smooth out the crumples of the **brown paper bag.** Dip your paintbrush in the colored water and remove any excess from the brush. Apply even and light strokes on the brown bag, being careful not to oversaturate the surface. Allow enough time for the bag to dry.

3. Once the bag is dry, rip into strips about 1½ inches wide, using a long metal ruler. Do not cut with scissors.

4. Turn one of the glass bowls upside down and cover with clear plastic wrap.

5. Dip the brown paper strips in the papier-mâché paste, being careful to remove any excess paste. Place on top of the plastic-covered glass bowl, covering it. Try to cover the bowl in one even layer.

6. Rip the **newspaper** into strips about 1½ inches wide. Dip the newspaper strips in the papier-mâché paste and place on top of the bowl, covering it. Try to cover the bowl in one even layer.

7. Repeat step 3 so that you have two layers of newspaper covering the bowl.

8. Apply one more layer of brown paper bag with papier-mâché paste.

9. Cover with clear plastic wrap.

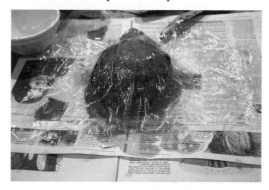

10. Take the second bowl, turn it upside down and place it on top of the first bowl. Allow the paste to dry overnight.

11. Once the paste is dry, remove the ceramic bowls and plastic wrap. Trim the edges.

12. Before putting any food inside the bowl, line it with a paper towel.

28. Sun Piñata

WITH ALL THOSE outdoor parties you've been throwing, doesn't it make sense to make this piñata? Almost all my friends have children who (1) like to eat candy, and (2) have the energy to swing a stick at a piñata until it's completely obliterated. And if you don't have kids, then you can make it an adult piñata. Pin a picture of someone's boss or ex-girlfriend/boyfriend on it and replace the candy with more adult treats, such as Godiva chocolate-covered espresso beans instead of M&M's.

Materials

5 empty toilet paper rolls
Masking tape
Large balloon

Newspaper
Papier-mâché paste (see page xvii)
Yellow tempera paint
Yellow tissue paper
White craft glue
Black and orange acrylic paint
Streamers
Lots o' candy
String
1 empty paper towel roll

Tools

Scissors   Serrated knife
Paintbrushes   Awl

Tip

- You can easily convert this sun into a sunflower. Simply change orange to green and add a stem at the bottom (a.k.a. paper towel roll).

Making the body of the sun

1. At the end of each **toilet paper roll,** form a point and hold together with masking tape.

2. With the pair of scissors, cut up the paper towel roll into four equal parts. At the end of each piece, form a point and hold together with masking tape.

3. Inflate the **balloon** to 7 or 8 inches in diameter. Tape the toilet paper rolls and paper towel roll pieces around the balloon so that the points are facing out. Alternate between the toilet paper rolls and paper towel roll pieces, and be sure to space them as evenly as possible.

4. Cut the **newspaper** into strips about 1½ inches wide. Dip the strips in the papier-mâché paste and place on top of the balloon and its toilet paper rolls. Be sure you have enough newspaper and paste to cover the balloon three times, but you only have to cover the toilet paper rolls once. This is the body of the sun. Allow enough time for the newspaper and paste to dry to the touch.

Decorating the body

5. Cover the entire body with **yellow tempera paint.** Allow enough time for the paint to dry before proceeding.

6. Cut the **tissue paper** in long strips approximately 2 inches wide.

7. Glue the tissue paper to the outside of the body using the **white craft glue.** Allow enough time for the glue to dry before proceeding.

8. Use the **black paint** to paint a face in the center of the body. Paint a scalloped border around the face, using the **orange paint.**

9. Tape the streamers to the ends of the sun's rays. See page 122 on how to make streamers.

Adding the candy

10. With the serrated knife, make a small U-shaped incision at the bottom of the body, about 1½ inches wide.

11. Gently pry open the incision and puncture the balloon if it has not already popped.

12. Place the **candy** inside the piñata.

13. Close the incision, using masking tape on the inside of the body.

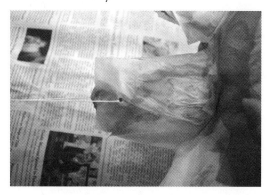

14. At topmost part of the piñata, punch a hole, using the awl. Be sure not to make the hole too close to the edge.

15. Thread the **string** through the hole and tie the piñata to a high tree branch or ceiling beam.

29. Pinwheel

ON THE FOURTH OF JULY, I've made a bunch of these for my kids and their friends. It's quick and easy, and I always have tons of material to use. It's based on a simple tea bag fold, which is similar to origami.

Materials

8 magazine sheets
Craft glue stick
1 chopstick or wooden paint mixing stick
1 paper clip
1 button
1 bead
1 small round plastic lid (from a sour cream or butter container)

Tools

Paper cutter
Awl
Chain-nose pliers

Tips

- Try to use magazine ads or covers instead of the regular pages because they are usually a bit thicker and more coated.

- When cutting up the sheets into 6-inch squares, pick the part of the sheet that has the most vibrant colors, patterns, or combination of both. Sometimes the printed words of the ad or cover can be distracting instead of adding to the overall design, so you might want to consider cutting those elements out of the square.

The folded unit

1. With the paper cutter, cut down the **magazine sheets** into 6-inch squares.

2. Take a square sheet and fold in half along the diagonal to form a triangle. Unfold. Fold along the opposite diagonal and unfold. You should have made an X with the creases of the two folds.

3. Fold the sheet in half by taking the top edge and bringing it to the bottom edge. Unfold. Fold in half again by taking the left edge and bringing it to the right edge. Unfold. You

should have made a plus sign with the creases of these two folds. The paper should look like this:

4. Turn the paper 45 degrees so that you have a diamond. Along the horizontal crease, fold in half by bringing the top point to the bottom, forming a triangle.

5. Take the left "arm" of your triangle and fold along the crease, down toward the bottom point. This is your first folded unit.

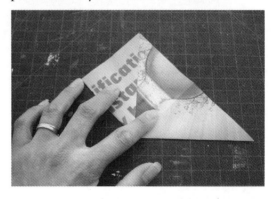

6. Repeat steps through until you have eight folded units.

7. Glue the units together, layering them, until you have this pattern:

The spinner

8. Apply glue to the center of the **plastic lid,** centered, on top of the folded unit. Wait a few minutes for the glue to dry.

9. Take the awl and poke a hole in the center of the lid.

10. Unwind the **paper clip** to form a straight line. With the chain-nose pliers, curve one end.

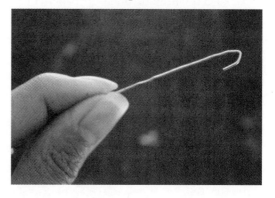

11. Attach the **button** to the curved end of the paper clip, essentially "weaving" it through two holes.

12. Push the other end of the paper clip through the hole in the lids until it reaches the button.

Putting it all together

13. Push the **bead** through the paper clip. Giving yourself ½-inch of slack from the bead, secure it by twisting the paper clip. Leave at least a 3-inch tail.

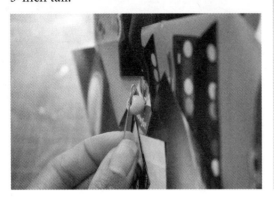

14. Wrap the remaining tail around the **wooden chopstick.**

30. Toy Dump Truck

THIS TOY DUMP TRUCK complements the sand toys made in the previous chapter, although I'm sure that you do not necessarily have to bring this truck to the beach to get any use out of it.

Materials

1 half-gallon milk or juice carton
Yellow duct tape, 3 inches wide
Black electrical tape, 1 inch wide
Metallic tape, 3 inches wide
Tacky glue
1 round plastic 16-ounce container
4 vitamin bottle caps
6 paper clips
4 buttons or beads

Tools

Binder clips   Craft knife
Ruler   Scissors
Fine-point marker   Awl

Tip

• Many half-gallon containers these days have a twist-off cap at the top. Incorporate it into your design by making it a way for the sand to be released, like a hopper car on a train.

The body

1. Use the **tacky glue** to reseal the top opening of the **half-gallon milk carton.** Keep it shut with binder clips. Allow enough time for the glue to dry.

2. Remove the binder clips. Place the carton on its side, the bottom on the left side and the top on the right. Be sure that the top of the carton that is facing you is the pointed side.

3. Measure and draw a horizontal line 2½ inches from the bottom edge. Measure and draw a vertical line 5 inches from the top point of the carton on the right side.

draw a horizontal line 2½ inches from the bottom edge. Measure and draw a vertical line 5 inches from the top point of the carton on the left side.

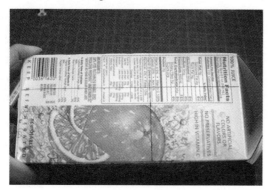

6. From the open right side, cut along the 2½-inch horizontal line. Stop at the 5-inch vertical line.

4. Cut off the bottom of the carton, using the craft knife. From the open left side, cut along the 2½-inch horizontal line. Stop at the 5-inch vertical line.

7. Roll the carton down once so that the flat side of the carton top is facing up. With the ruler and fine-point marker, draw a vertical line that connects the two 5-inch vertical lines on the

5. Flip the carton from right to left so that the pointed top is on the left side. Measure and

side. Cut along this vertical line until you are able to remove that piece of the carton.

8. With yellow duct tape, completely cover the carton. You may have to do two layers of duct tape so the graphics on the carton are not visible. This is the main body of the truck. Decorate the body further with the black electrical tape and metallic tape.

The wheels

9. With the awl, poke a hole in the center of each of the four bottle caps.

10. Straighten the four **paper clips.** With the chain-nose pliers, make one end of each paper clip into a T. Add a small **bead** to each paper clip.

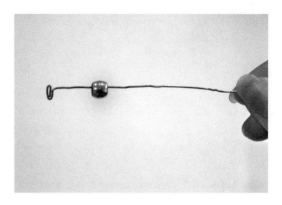

11. Poke two pairs of holes (two holes on each side) in the truck body, ¼ inch from the bottom edge. Try to make the two pairs of holes line up with each other.

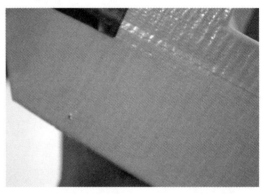

12. Starting from the inside of the truck body, push a paper clip through one of the holes all the way through until the bead is against the side.

13. On the other side, attach a bottle cap, the underside facing out, to the paper clip. With the chain-nose pliers, twist the end of the paper clip to secure the wheel.

14. Repeat steps 12 and 13 with the remaining paper clip/beads and bottle caps.

The loader

15. With the awl, poke a hole ¾ inch from the bottom edge of the round plastic container.

16. On both sides of the truck body, measure and mark a point 2¼ inches from the back edge and ½ inch from the top edge using the fine-point marker. Poke a hole through the points with the awl.

17. Straighten the two remaining paper clips and make a T at one end. Take the plastic container and align the hole with one of the holes on the side of the truck body. From the outside, push one of the paper clips through both holes until the T is flush against the outside of the truck body.

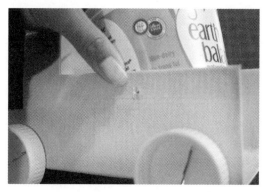

18. On the other side of the truck body and using the hole as your guide, poke a hole on the other side of plastic container. Push the last paper clip through until the T is flush against the outside of the truck body. Inside the plastic container, twist the two ends of the paper clips together and wrap with duct tape.

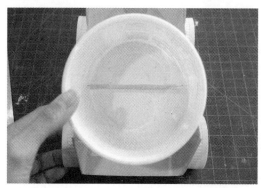

August

Projects This Month

Shell Fragment Necklace

T-Shirt Throw Pillows

Shell Picture Frame

Rock Animals

AUGUST IS A VERY LAZY MONTH. In fact, there's a special day in August dedicated to *being* lazy. Ah, yes, it's the time of the year when sitting on our laurels is the only activity that does not make us sweat—and that's because we're on a beach.

Speaking of beaches, my kids like to think they are going to use every darn thing they find on Mother Nature's sandy shores. Although I try to return most of it, there's always a hidden stash of treasures stowed away in some remote part of the car. When I find it, I don't despair. I just think of all the things I can make—albeit at a much slower pace than usual (did I mention August was a lazy month?).

The crafts this month are quick and easy, so you can go back to doing all things lazy.

Materials you will need this month

Shell fragment

Black leather string, 4 feet

1 metallic bead

Lots of young children's T-shirts

Thread

Old pillow or bag of poly-fill

2 old ponytail elastics or scrunchies

Embroidery floss

A 5 × 7-inch wood or plastic picture frame

Brown paper grocery bag, undone at the seams

Lots of shells

Sand

A whole lot of rocks

Hard bristles from a brush

August holidays, typical and not-so

Friendship Day (1st)
National Ice-Cream Sandwich Day (1st)
National Watermelon Day (3rd)
Twins Day Festival (4th)
National Mustard Day (5th)
Wiggle Your Toes Day (6th)
National Polka Festival (9th)
Lazy Day (10th)
Middle Child's Day (12th)
Blame Someone Else Day (13th)
National Failures Day (15th)
National Thrift Shop Day (17th)
Bad Poetry Day (18th)
National Radio Day (20th)
National Spongecake Day (23rd)
Kiss-and-Make-Up Day (25th)
National Cherry Popsicle Day (26th)
World Sauntering Day (28th)
National Toasted Marshmallow Day (30th)
National Trail Mix Day (31st)

Monthlong celebrations

National Catfish Month
National Golf Month
National Eye Exam Month
National Water Quality Month
Romance Awareness Month
Peach Month
Foot Health Month

August birthdays of famous people

Francis Scott Key (1st)
Tony Bennett (3rd)
Louis Armstrong (4th)
Neil Armstrong (5th)
Andy Warhol (6th)
Herbert Hoover (10th)
Alex Haley (11th)
Cecil B. DeMille (12th)
Alfred Hitchcock (13th)
Madonna (16th)
Mae West (17th)
Davy Crockett (17th)
Robert Redford (18th)
William Jefferson Clinton (19th)
Orville Wright (19th)
H. P. Lovecraft (20th)
Benjamin Harrison (20th)
Count Basie (21st)
Ray Bradbury (22nd)
Dorothy Parker (22nd)
Leonard Bernstein (25th)
Mother Teresa (26th)
Lyndon B. Johnson (27th)
Elizabeth Ann Seton (28th)
Charlie "Bird" Parker (29th)

31. Shell Fragment Necklace

THE SEARCH for that perfect shell can be daunting. More often than not, you'll come across a piece of a shell with brilliant colors and interesting shapes. So why look further? A fragment can be more interesting and can masquerade as a semiprecious stone or quartz. All it takes is a little imagination and some mineral oil to polish the shell.

Materials

Shell fragment
Black leather string, 4 feet
1 metallic bead

Tools

Cotton rag or   Awl
  paper towel   Mineral oil
Pin tool

Tip

• Certain shells are more dense than others. Try using oyster shells, which are a bit softer and easier to carve into.

Preparing the shell fragment

1. Wipe a little mineral oil onto the shell, then wipe clean with a cotton rag or paper towel.

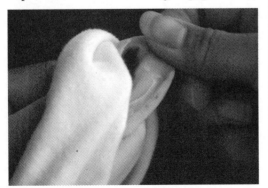

2. With a pin tool, carefully begin carving a small hole ⅛ to ¼-inch from the edge of the shell.

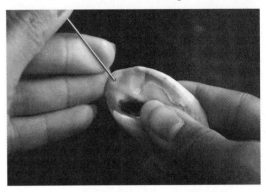

3. Once you have a small groove, switch to the awl. Carefully and slowly carve into the shell until you are able to push the awl through to the other side.

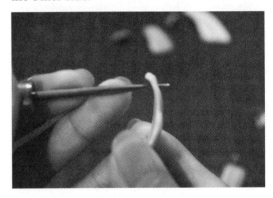

Attaching the pieces

4. Fold the **black leather string** in half. Push the folded end through the hole in the shell from the back, exposing a small loop through the front.

Little Notepad

Rolled Bead Bracelet

"Sock" Monkey

Little Wallet

Cardboard House

February

LOVE
Embroidered Card

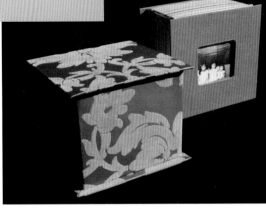

Keepsake Box

Paper Dolls

March

Window Planter

Toy Boat

Toy Car

Picture Mobile

Cherry Blossom
Greeting Card

Bear Doll

Garden Butterflies

Paper Flowers

Mother's Day Card

Handbag

June

Father's Day Card

Sun Hat

July

Outdoor Serving Bowls

Sun Piñata

Pinwheel

Toy Dump Truck

Shell Fragment Necklace

T-Shirt Throw Pillows

Rock Animals

Shell Picture Frame

September

Chihuahua
Greeting Card

Pencil Case

Rocket Key Chain

October

Ghosts on a String

Train Engine
Costume

Bat Mobile

November

Thanksgiving Wreath

Crayon Candle

Brown Bag
Coasters

December

Holiday Cracker

Holiday Card

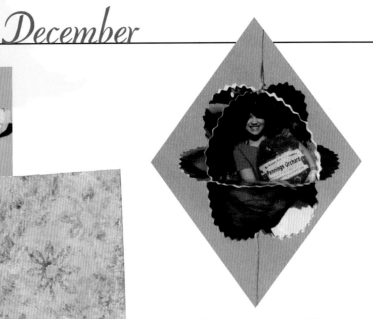

Photo Ornament Ball

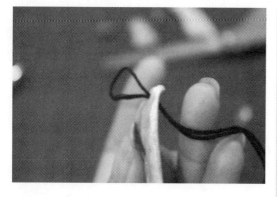

5. Take the two loose ends of the string and push them through the loop.

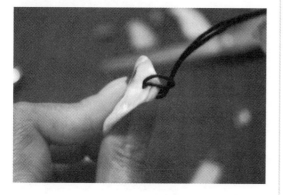

8. Push down the bead so it rests above the shell fragment. Knot the string above the bead.

6. Gently pull the loose ends of the string until the loop is closed.

Getting the proper length

9. To measure how long you want your necklace to be, take the loose ends of the string and tie a loose knot.

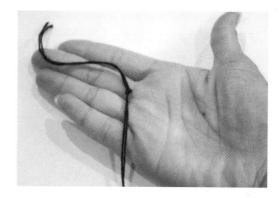

7. Add the **metallic bead,** threading both sides of the string through it.

10. Place the necklace around your neck and see where the shell fragment falls against your chest. Adjust the knot until you get the desired length, then secure the knot so it will not fall apart.

32. T-Shirt Throw Pillows

My daughter loves her things to a fault. The "blankie" she had since birth has been on its last legs for quite some time now, and the many T-shirts my husband picked up for her on his various business trips still inhabit her dresser despite being four sizes too small.

While she will never let go of her precious blankie, I've been allowed to make a pillow or two from all those T-shirts.

Materials

Lots of young children's T-shirts
Thread
Old pillow or bag of poly-fill
2 old ponytail elastics or scrunchies
Embroidery floss

Tools

Scissors
Sewing needles, regular and large

Tip

• You can embroider your child's name on the front of the pillow, or add decorative stitched border around any design on the T-shirt.

Small rectangle throw pillow

1. Lay one T-shirt flat on your work surface. Cut a rectangle around the printed graphic on the front of the shirt. Be sure to cut the front and the back of the shirt so you have two layers.

2. Flip the two layers over and place them on top of each other.

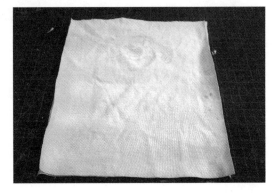

3. Thread your needle and begin sewing the two layers together at the edges.

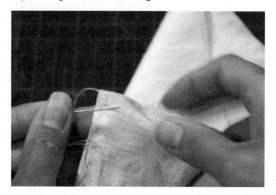

4. Once you've sewn three sides, turn it inside out and stuff the inside with the contents of the old pillow.

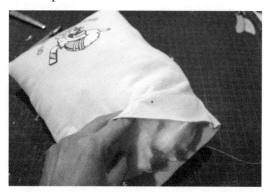

5. Sew the last side closed.

Double-sided pillow

6. Lay two T-shirts flat on your work surface. Cut out the front sides of each T-shirt and discard the rest.

7. Take the smaller shirt piece. Try to cut a rectangle with the printed graphic centered. Then place it on top of the second shirt piece, aligning the printed graphics of both shirt pieces. Cut the second shirt piece to match the size of the first shirt piece.

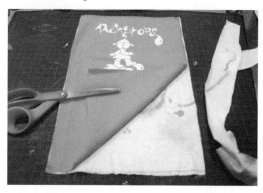

8. Flip the first shirt piece over so that the printed graphic sides of both shirt pieces are facing each other. Thread your needle and begin sewing the two shirt pieces together at the edges.

9. Repeat steps 4 and 5.

Patchwork tube pillow

10. Cut four T-shirts into sixteen 6-inch squares.

11. Sew the squares together from the back, making a patchwork with four rows and four columns of squares. It should measure approximately 23½ × 23½ inches.

12. Fold the patchwork in half, the seamed side exposed, so the top and bottom edges are touching. Sew the top and bottom edges to

form a tube pillowcase. Turn the tube inside out and begin stuffing.

13. Secure one **ponytail elastic** at one end of the tube pillow, approximately 4 inches from the edge. Finish stuffing the pillow and then secure the second ponytail elastic on the remaining end, approximately 4 inches from the edge.

14. With the larger needle and embroidery thread, sew a blanket stitch (see page xvii) at the two edges of the pillow.

33. Shell Picture Frame

EVER SINCE I GOT MARRIED, picture frames have been given to me on various gift-giving occasions. Fortunately, I have a lot of photos that I like to display. Unfortunately, none of my frames seem to complement one another.

Here is a way to disguise a frame that otherwise would not see the light of day. With a little glue and a lot of shells, you can cover up either a really plain frame or one that is not quite your style. If you don't have any shells, try using small rocks or sea glass.

Materials

5 × 7-inch wood picture frame
Brown paper grocery bag, undone at the seams
Lots of shells
White craft glue
Sand
Medium glaze

Tools

Pencil
Painter's tape,
  blue or purple

Small plastic bowl
  or cup
1-inch paintbrush

Tip

• If you are trying to cover a metal frame, you will need to first cover it with rice paper, which is thin yet strong. Apply a thin layer of glue with a brush and then add the rice paper. With a dry brush, push down the paper onto the glue.

Covering the frame

1. Remove glass and backing from the frame.

2. With the pencil, trace the outline of the frame onto the **brown paper bag.** Inside the outline, arrange the shells as you would want them on

the frame. Place them as close as possible to one another.

3. Clean the frame of all dirt and dust. Cover the glass with painter's tape. Set aside.

4. Add glue to one section of the frame, adding the shells as they correlate to the arrangement on the brown paper bag. Do one section at a time.

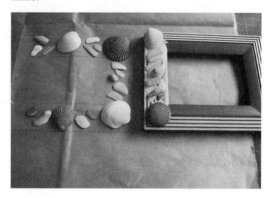

5. Once all the shells are on the frame, add glue to the spaces in between.

6. Sprinkle the sand evenly over the frame, making sure to cover all the spaces between the shells. Allow time for the glue to dry.

7. Once the glue is dry, gently shake off the excess sand.

8. Add a thick layer of glaze over the shells and sand. Allow time for the glaze to dry.

9. Once the glaze is dry, remove the painter's tape.

34. Rock Animals

DO YOUR KIDS pick up rocks wherever they go? Sure, they call it a "rock collection," but you know better. In my own kids' collection of rocks, I've spotted petrified wood, interesting pieces of concrete, and sea glass along with true rocks of every color and texture.

I usually make my kids give up portions of their vast collection when rocks are more of a presence than living beings. Sometimes I use their rocks to decorate our outdoor garden. Other times, I just can't help myself and make these rock animals.

The instructions are pretty much the same for all the rock animals, which is to glue the rocks together and move on. So instead of repeating myself, I've given you pictures of some rock animals I've made. As they say, imitation is the best form of flattery, so imitate away.

Materials

A whole lot of rocks
Tacky glue

Tools

Hard-bristle brush
Paintbrushes
Paint

Tips

- Sometimes the rocks can be either too heavy or too light to complete your animal in one sitting. You may need to assemble parts of the animal first, allow time to dry, and then put it all together at a later time. Be patient and try to plan the order in which the parts will be put together.

- Before you start glueing the rocks, make sure they are clean. Using the hard-bristle brush, scrub the rocks free from dirt. Rinse with water if necessary.

Turtle

Dog

Elephant

Giraffe

September

Projects This Month

Paper Rocket Key Chain

Pop-Up Chihuahua Greeting Card

Candy Wrapper Pencil Case

Duct Tape School Folder

SEPTEMBER BRINGS US LABOR DAY, the end of summer, the beginning of autumn, back to school, and the start of apple-picking season. But what my kids look forward to the most is all that new stuff: the school supplies, the fall wardrobe, the new shoes and backpacks.

We have this tradition of making something for school, something that we can usually buy but choose to make. The consummate spin master that I am, I say that it's a way to have something that no one else will have, a wholly unique thing that all the other kids will be asking, "where did you get *that?*" And my kids eat it up, for what is adolescence but the time in which youngsters are constantly trying to be different than everyone else? Oh, I may be guilty for playing on a child's vanity, but if it saves a tree or a river . . .

My kids personalize their things with items that they have collected: a street map of a place they visited during the summer, tickets from a show they loved, or wrappers of their favorite candy. I try to plan out what they are going to make at least a month in advance so we can save the appropriate items. Sometimes it can literally be a sticky situation, though. (My son once decided to save bottle caps, but neglected to wash them. You can only imagine how this affected our already burgeoning ant problem.) So be sure to wash anything that may need washing, and store these items in sealable bags—just in case.

Materials you will need this month

1 brown paper grocery bag or used gift wrap

2 small paper clips

1 large paper clip

1 plastic bread or newspaper bag

Lots of thin white cardboard (T-shirt inserts and bedding packaging)

6 large cereal boxes

1 roll red duct tape, approximately 2 inches wide

Candy wrappers

3 thick thread velcro tabs

2 large cereal boxes

Duct tape (any color)

September holidays, typical and not-so

Skyscraper Day (3rd)

Be Late For Something Day (5th)

Labor Day (1st Monday)

Fight Procrastination Day (6th)

Neither Rain nor Snow Day (7th)

National Date Nut Bread Day (8th)

Swap Ideas Day (10th)

National Chocolate Milkshake Day (12th)

Defy Superstition Day (13th)

National Cream-filled Donut Day (14th)

Felt Hat Day (15th)

Collect Rocks Day (16th)

National Apple Dumpling Day (17th)

National Play-Doh Day (18th)

National Butterscotch Pudding Day (19th)

First Day of Autumn (21st–24th [check calendar])

Rosh Hashanah and Yom Kippur (check calendar; can also occur in October)

Hobbit Day (22nd)

Festival of Latest Novelties (24th)

National Comic Book Day (25th)

National Good Neighbor Day (26th)

Crush a Can Day (27th)

Ask a Stupid Question Day (28th)

Monthlong celebrations

Self-Improvement Month

Be Kind to Editors and Writers Month

International Square Dance Month

Cable TV Month

National Bed Check Month

National Chicken Month

National Courtesy Month

National Honey Month

National Mind Mapping Month

National Piano Month

National Rice Month

National Papaya Month

Classical Music Month

Christa McAuliffe (2nd)
Jesse James (5th)
Roger Waters (6th)
Grandma Moses (7th)
D. H. Lawrence (11th)
O. Henry (11th)
Jesse Owens (12th)
Roald Dahl (13th)
William H. Taft (15th)
Lauren Bacall (16th)
Greta Garbo (18th)
Upton Sinclair (20th)

Stephen King (21st)
H. G. Wells (21st)
Ray Charles (23rd)
John Coltrane (23rd)
F. Scott Fitzgerald (24th)
Shel Silverstein (25th)
William Faulkner (25th)
George Gershwin (26th)
T. S. Eliot (26th)
Ed Sullivan (28th)
Truman Capote (30th)

35. Paper Rocket Key Chain

KEY CHAINS have become more of an accessory than the utilitarian item that simply held keys. I have kids that like to hang key chains off their backpack as if they were charms on a bracelet. At the local candy store, the proprietor annoyingly displays his key chains for sale at the cash register, where swarms of children beg their parents for one with the latest miniature Monopoly or Twister, or the mini Maglite or the (gasp!) glass-encased cigarette.

I've made this rocket key chain to rival the store-bought trifles my children are willing to spend their allowance on.

Materials

1 brown paper grocery bag or used gift wrap
White glue
3 small paper clips
1 large paper clip
Acrylic paint
Glaze
1 plastic bread or newspaper bag

Tools

Metal ruler,
   24 inches long
Craft knife
Bamboo skewer
Pin tool

Awl
Round-nose pliers
Chain-nose pliers
Fine paintbrushes

Tip

• These rocket key chains do fly through the air fairly well. So be sure not to skimp on the streamer at the end.

The main body of the ship

1. Using the metal ruler and craft knife, cut a triangular piece from the **brown paper bag,** 2 inches wide at the base and 24 inches from the base to the point.

2. Add a thin stream of **glue** to the back of the triangle. Be sure to leave ¾ inch at the wide end of the triangle glue-free.

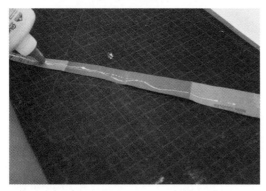

3. Starting at the wide end of the triangle, roll the triangle around the bamboo skewer until you have a very large paper bead. This is the main body of the rocket.

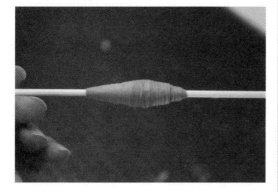

The legs

4. About ½ inch from the bottom edge of the main body, poke a hole all the way through

with the pin tool. If you are unable to push all the way through, try using the awl.

5. Rotate the main body 90 degrees. Repeat step 4. You should now have four holes ½ inch from the bottom edge of the main body, each approximately ¼ inch away from one another.

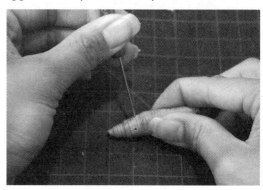

6. Straighten two of the small **paper clips.** Push them through the holes of the main body.

7. With the round-nose pliers, curl the ends of the paper clips so they form legs for the main body to stand on.

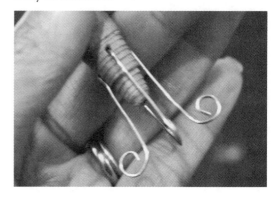

The key chain and streamer

8. Straighten the **large paper clip.** Fold it 2 inches from one end, forming a right angle.

9. With the round-nose and chain-nose pliers, form a circle approximately ¼ inch in diameter at the folded end of the paper clip.

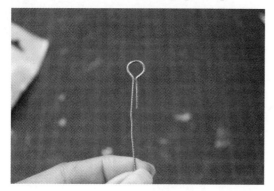

10. From the bottom opening of the rocket's main body (near the legs), insert the large paper clip. Push it as far as it can go, with the small circle end flush against the bottom opening.

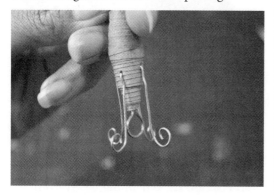

11. At the top opening of the rocket's main body, the remaining end of the large paper clip should be exposed. Make a circle at the end of the paper clip, approximately ¼ inch in diameter. Try to come as close as possible to the top opening of the rocket's main body.

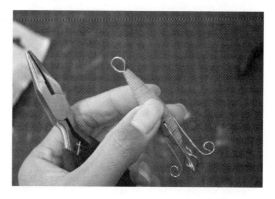

12. Take the last small paper clip and curl it into a circle ½ to ¾ inch in diameter. Be sure the ends overlap. Attach this circle to the top of the main body.

13. Paint the main body with the **acrylic paint.** After the paint dries, add a coat of **glaze.**

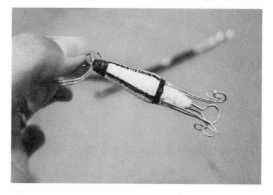

14. Cut a long, thin strip of **plastic bag,** approximately ¼ inch wide and 24 inches long. This is the streamer. Tie the streamer to the bottom of the rocket.

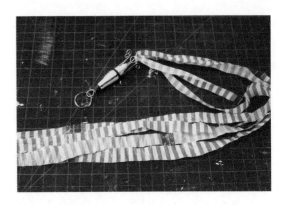

36. Pop-Up Chihuahua Greeting Card

ONCE SCHOOL BEGINS, it seems as if we're inundated with birthday party invitations. The summer reprieve is officially over, so get ready to par-tay!

This is a fun pop-up card that gets a lot of attention. I've made this one for a particular dog-loving friend of my daughter's, who liked the card more than any other card—or gift, for that matter. And it's a Chihuahua—who doesn't like a Chihuahua?

Materials

Lots of thin white cardboard (T-shirt inserts and bedding packaging)
White glue

Tools

Paper cutter Scissors
Roll of duct tape Bone folder
Pencil Metal ruler
Craft knife

Tip

• If you don't have any T-shirt inserts or bed linen packaging, try using food boxes that are printed on thin white cardboard.

Base card

1. Using the paper cutter, cut out two 5½ × 8½-inch rectangles. Fold in half to 5½ × 4½ inches. These are your base cards. Set one base card aside.

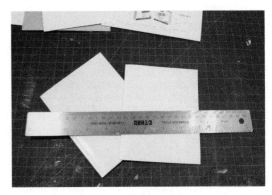

2. Position the remaining base card in the portrait format, with the card opening at the right side. Open the card so the inside left and right panels are facing you.

3. Take the roll of duct tape and center it on top of the open base card. Push down the roll so it is approximately 1 inch from the bottom edge. With a pencil, trace the inner circle of the roll onto the base card.

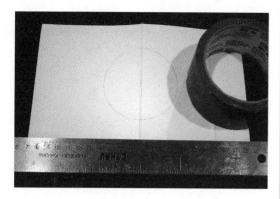

The ears, snout, and jaw

4. Photocopy the templates of the ears, upper snout, and lower jaw *at 200 percent.* Use the scissors to cut out the photocopied templates.

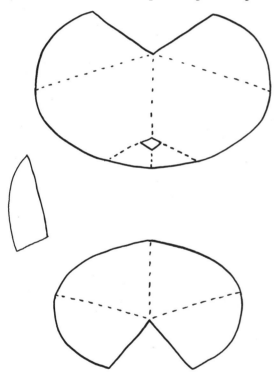

5. Take the piece of white cardboard. Be sure you have a piece that, when folded, measures at least 5 inches (folded side) × 3 inches. Align the upper snout and lower jaw templates along the folded edge and trace them.

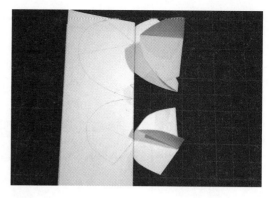

6. Cut out the shapes of the upper snout and lower jaw from the folded cardboard. Fold where indicated on the template and mark the tops and bottoms lightly with pencil.

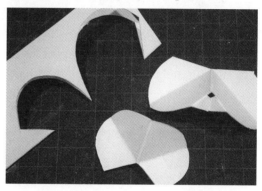

7. Trace the ear template on the remaining folded cardboard and cut out the shape. Be sure to cut through two layers so you yield two ears. The shape of the template is the left ear; the flopped version is the right ear. Mark them accordingly with your pencil.

8. Place the snout on the base card so the middle creases are on top of each other. Position the left side of the snout inside the boundaries of the upper left portion of the circle.

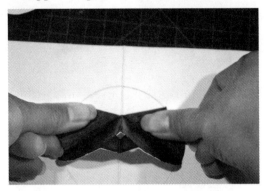

9. Place an index finger on the upper left panel of the snout. Lift up the rest of the snout at the crease. Trace the line of the crease onto the base card. Remove the snout.

10. Fold the base card along the middle crease so that the inside panels are exposed and the left side is facing up. Take the lower jaw and nest it against the folded side of the base card. Push down the lower jaw so the bottom point of the fold touches the bottom of the circle on the base card. Tilt the lower jaw to the right so the left point of the crease is inside the boundaries of the circle.

11. Place an index finger on the upper portion of the jaw and lift up the rest of the jaw at the crease. Trace the line of the crease onto the base card. Remove the jaw.

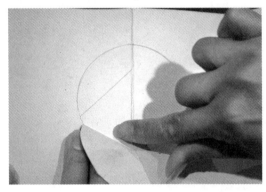

12. Place the left ear about ¾ inch from the folded edge, along the outline of the circle. Trace the bottom edge of the ear onto the base card and remove the ear.

13. The three lines drawn onto the base card are the entry slits for attaching the snout, lower jaw, and ears. With the craft knife, cut these three lines deeply so you get through both panels of the card. Be sure to avoid extending your slits all the way to the folded edge of the base card.

14. Open up the base card and attach the snout, lower jaw, and ears. Push in the nose of the snout.

15. Turn the card over and glue down the panels of the pieces to the card.

16. Take the second base card and glue it on top. Smooth down with a bone folder. Decorate the front panel of the card and the Chihuahua.

37. Candy Wrapper Pencil Case

THIS CASE can hold pencils, pens, eraser, and candy, too. Just make sure there isn't too much candy in there.

Materials

"The mix" (see page xvi)
2 large cereal boxes
1 roll of red duct tape, approximately 2 inches wide
Candy wrappers
Thick thread
3 velcro tabs

Tools

1-inch paintbrush	Metal ruler
Bone folder	Thick sewing needle
Paper cutter	Awl
Craft knife	Scissors

Tip

• Try using candy boxes, too (Mike & Ike, Milk Duds). You can sew pretty much anything to the front, as long as you prepunch the sewing holes with an awl.

The boards

1. With a brush, apply a thin layer of **"the mix"** to one side of one **cereal box.** Place the sec-

ond cereal box on top and smooth out air pockets with the bone folder. Allow time for the adhesive to dry.

2. Once the adhesive is dry, cut down the boxes into two 8½ × 5-inch, one 8½ × 2-inch, and one 8½ × 1-inch rectangular pieces. These are the boards.

The outer cover

3. Cut seven strips of **duct tape** approximately 16 inches long. Piece them together, overlapping them along the long side ⅛ to ¼ inch, with the sticky side facing up. In the end you have one large piece that is approximately 12 × 16 inches.

4. Along the left edge, place the metal ruler (metal side facing down) vertically as close to the edge as possible, as straight as you can.

5. Take the 8½ × 2-inch board and align the 2-inch side along the edge of the metal ruler. Place it on top of the duct tape, approximately ½ inch from the top.

6. Take one of the 8½ × 5-inch boards and align the 5-inch side along the edge of the metal ruler. Place it on top of the duct tape, approximately 1¼ inches below the first board.

7. Take the 8½ × 1-inch board and align the 1-inch side along the edge of the metal ruler. Place it on top of the duct tape, approximately ⅛ inch below the second board.

8. Take the last 8½ × 5-inch board and align the 5-inch side along the edge of the metal ruler. Place it on top of the duct tape, approximately ⅛ inch below the third board.

9. Remove the metal ruler. At each corner, cut off the excess duct tape at a 45-degree angle approximately ⅛ inch from the tip. Pull the duct tape tightly over only the top and bottom edges of the boards. Leave the sides undone. This is the outer cover.

Putting it all together

10. Flip over the outer cover. The top panel is the cover flap (upside down). The second panel is the back, the third panel is the bottom, and the fourth panel is the front (upside down).

11. Take the **candy wrappers** and decide where you want to sew them. Use a thick sewing needle and linen thread. Prepunch the holes with the awl before sewing.

12. Flip the outer cover over. On the left and right side of the third panel, or bottom, cut out triangular slits like the picture below:

13. Take the fourth panel, or the front, and bring it up, folding it over so it is at the same height as the second panel, or the back.

14. Take the excess duct tape at the side of the panels and push them together. This is the pencil case.

15. Add duct tape to the inside of the pencil case.

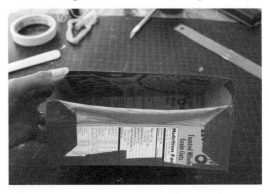

16. Add the Velcro tabs to the inside of the cover flap.

38. Duct Tape School Folder

AT THE BEGINNING of every school year, the color coded folders are at the top of the supply list sent to you from your child's teacher: Red, Yellow, Green, and Blue, each relating to a particular subject. I once stood on line at the local office supply store for over an hour to purchase these silly two-dollar folders because I didn't think there was a better way. Well, one day I was at our local hardware store and came upon the most beautiful sight: duct tape in red, yellow, green, and blue. Life has never been the same.

Materials

"The mix" (see page xvi)
4 large cereal boxes
Duct tape (any color)

Tools

1-inch brush   Paper cutter
Bone folder   Scissors

Tip

- If you don't have enough cereal boxes to double the boards, you can omit that part. But be sure to apply "the mix" as thinly as possible to avoid any warping or curling.

The boards

1. With a brush, apply a thin layer of "the mix" to one side of one **cereal box.** Place the second cereal box on top and smooth out air pockets with the bone folder. Allow time for the adhesive to dry. Repeat.

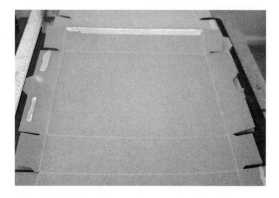

2. Once the adhesive is dry, use the paper cutter to cut down the boxes into two 9⅜ × 11½-inch and two 8⅞ × 5-inch rectangular pieces. These are the boards.

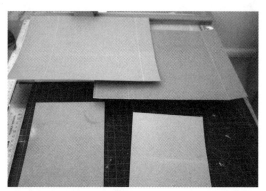

The outer cover

3. Cut eight strips of duct tape approximately 20 inches long. Piece them together, overlapping them along the long side ⅛ to ¼ inch, and with

the sticky side facing up. In the end you have one large piece that is approximately 13¼ × 20 inches.

4. Along the bottom edge, place the metal ruler (metal side facing down) horizontally as close to the edge as possible, as straight as you can.

5. Take one of the 9⅜ × 11½-inch boards and align the 9⅜-inch side along the edge of the metal ruler. Place it on top of the duct tape, approximately ½ inch from the left edge.

6. Take the other 9⅜ × 11½-inch board and align the 9⅜-inch side along the edge of the metal ruler. Place it on top of the duct tape, approximately 1⁄16 inch to the right of the first board. This is the outer cover of the folder.

7. Remove the metal ruler. Cut off the excess duct tape at the four corners. Be sure to cut at a 45-degree angle approximately ⅛ inch from the tip.

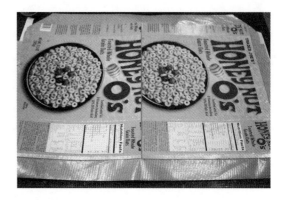

8. Take the two 8⅞ × 5-inch boards and place each of them on top of the larger boards. Align the outer corners and bottom edges.

9. Pull the duct tape over the edges on all four sides.

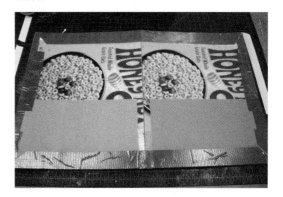

10. With a craft knife, carefully cut the duct tape only at the following creases in the picture:

11. Cut a piece of duct tape approximately 11 inches long.

12. Place the tape over the center crease inside the folder.

October

Projects This Month

Train Engine Costume

Cat Costume

Fairy Wings

Family of Ghosts on a String

Paper Bat Mobile

OCTOBER IS ONE OF MY FAVORITE MONTHS, with brilliantly colored foliage that would make anyone pause in introspective revelation. The weather is a perfect mix of sunny skies and crispy air. Throwing on a pair of well-worn jeans and a comfy sweater is what most of us have been looking forward to after a season of trying to keep pretty toes and even tans. Plus the lack of humidity means weeks and weeks of good hair—how can anyone argue with that?

And I still get a little giddy anticipating Halloween at the end of the month. Before I had my own, I use to borrow my sister's kids on Halloween, thinking that once you become old enough to drive, going trick-or-treating would make you an opportunist for free stuff. But not true. Aside from the whole candy overload aspect of this holiday, Halloween is a chance to become a kid again, get into a costume, and become a free spirit. Other people expect this from you, too. So why disappoint?

Materials you will need this month

1 large corrugated box (large enough for a young child to wear)

Tacky glue

1 screw eye

1 plastic bread or newspaper bag

Acrylic paint

1 pair old stockings (adult size)

1 small piece pink felt, 3 × 5 inches

1 sleeping mask

1 pair black tights or thick stockings (adult size)

1 black T-shirt (adult size)

Black thread

1 skein hairy or fuzzy black yarn

4 pairs hooks and eyes from an old skirt or blouse

6 bamboo skewers, 12 inches long

Yellow duct tape (2-inch-wide roll)

2 small paper clips

Newspaper

1 empty paper towel roll

1 pair stockings (adult size)

4 white garbage bags

4 pieces twine or string, approximately 2 feet long

1 tie

1 wig

1 skein yarn

2 baseball caps

4 paper clips

1 long piece twine, 8 feet long

Used 8½ × 11-inch printer paper or other white paper ready for the recycle bin

Black watercolor paint

1 roll nylon string

1 screw eye

String, 4 feet

October holidays, typical and not-so

World Vegetarian Day (1st)

National Golf Day (4th)

National Storytelling Festival (5th)

Moldy Cheese Day (9th)

It's My Party Day (11th)

International Moment of Frustration Scream Day (12th)

National Peanut Festival (13th)

Be Bald and Free Day (14th)

Columbus Day (second Monday in October)

Dictionary Day (16th)

No Beard Day (18th)

Evaluate Your Life Day (19th)

Babbling Day (21st)

National Nut Day (22nd)

National Bologna Day (24th)

Punk for a Day Day (25th)

Sylvia Plath Day (27th)

National Chocolate Day (28th)

National Candy Corn Day (30th)

Halloween and National Magic Day (31st)

Monthlong celebrations

Adopt-a-Dog Month
Computer Learning Month
National Apple Jack Month
National Car Care Month
National Clock Month
National Cosmetology Month
National Dessert Month
Family History Month
National Pickled Pepper Month

National Pizza Month
National Popcorn Poppin' Month
National Pretzel Month
National Roller Skating Month
National Sarcastics Month
National Seafood Month
National Stamp Collecting Month
National Kitchen and Bath Month
Vegetarian Awareness Month

October birthdays of famous people

Jimmy Carter (1st)
Mahatma Gandhi (2nd)
Rutherford B. Hayes (4th)
Chester A. Arthur (5th)
George Westinghouse (6th)
John Lennon (9th)
Helen Hayes (10th)
Eleanor Roosevelt (11th)
Paul Simon (13th)
E. E. cummings (14th)
Dwight Eisenhower (14th)
William Penn (14th)
Eugene O'Neill (16th)
Oscar Wilde (16th)

Noah Webster (16th)
Arthur Miller (17th)
Art Buchwald (20th)
Dizzy Gillespie (21st)
Alfred Nobel (21st)
Johnny Carson (23rd)
Pablo Picasso (25th)
Dylan Thomas (27th)
Theodore Roosevelt (27th)
Ezra Pound (30th)
John Adams (30th)
Juliette Low (31st)

39. Train Engine Costume

A CORRUGATED BOX is fodder for a child's imagination. When our new washing machine arrived, the large brown corrugated box was a playhouse for weeks, occupying a space in our backyard underneath the Japanese maple tree. My kids kept a tin of markers and a pad of paper inside, and decorated the inner walls with drawings. We cut out windows and a doorway, and they played for hours until their fingers turned numb from the cold. When we finally threw it out, the kids were sad to see it go.

I took a cue from this experience and now save all my corrugated boxes. Sometimes we get lucky and get one large enough for a playhouse, but more often we get boxes that are not big enough. So we make costumes: a boat, a car, a robot. This is a train that my son wore with pride during our village's annual Halloween parade.

Materials

1 large corrugated box (large enough for a
    young child to wear)
Tacky glue
1 screw eye
1 plastic bread or newspaper bag
Acrylic paint
1 pair of old stockings (adult size)

Tools

Scissors   Bone folder
Pencil   Craft knife
Small hand weights   Paintbrushes
Metal ruler, 24 inches
    long

Tip

• If your child wants to be the train engineer, dress him or her in overalls and a bandana.

The cowcatcher

1. With the scissors, cut off three of the bottom flaps from the **corrugated box,** leaving one short flap intact. Set the flaps aside.

2. Take the remaining bottom flap and fold it out. Measure and mark a parallel line 2½ inches from where it attaches to the box. Score and fold up toward the box.

3. Measure and mark a parallel line 3½ inches from the first line. Score and fold up toward the box.

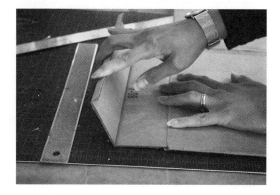

4. You should have three panels. When folded, it should make a triangle. Press the last—and smallest—panel against the surface of the box. Use the **tacky glue** to glue it in place. This is the cowcatcher.

Reinforcing the sides of the main body

5. On the top of the box, cut off the long side flaps and glue them to the inside of the box. You might need to do them one at a time and weigh it down with a hand weight. Allow time for one side to dry before proceeding to the next step.

The smokestack

6. Take the short top flap that is on the same side as the cowcatcher. Take one of the long flaps that you removed from the bottom and glue it to the inside of the short flap so that it is standing straight up. Try to center it as much as possible. Again, you might have to use a hand weight to hold the flaps together while

they dry. Place the box on the edge of your worktable and allow enough time for the glue to dry before proceeding to the next step.

7. Once the glue is dry, lightly draw a 4 × 3-inch rectangle centered at the top of the flap. The top of the rectangle should be flush with the top of the flap.

8. Cut off the excess parts at the left and right of the rectangle. This is your smokestack.

The car connector

9. Take the remaining long flap that you removed from the bottom. Place it in on top of train body's back side. Mark off the width of the train body on the long flap.

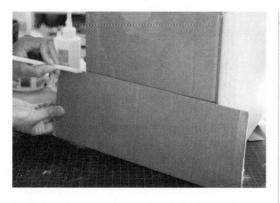

10. Fold in the opposite ends of the long flap to match the width of train body. Measure 1 inch out from the fold on each side and fold again.

11. Glue to bottom of train body's back side. Be sure it is flush to the train body's bottom edge. This is the car connector. You may need large binder clips to hold the car connector in place. Allow enough time for the glue to dry before proceeding to the next step.

12. Add the **screw eye** to the car connector. Cut up the **plastic bread bag** to make a few streamers (see page 122) and tie them on.

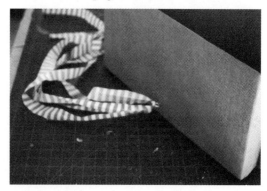

Adding the details

13. Cut off the remaining short flap at the top of the train body. Paint the entire train body a solid color. Add the details: a circle on the front side for the engine, grill lines on the cow-catcher, windows all around the body, and your child's name on the back.

14. Cut two small holes on each side of the train body. Cut off the legs of the **stockings** and insert one leg per train body side. Knot the ends of the stockings. These are the straps.

40. Cat Costume

A FEW TIMES I've had the distinct pleasure of taking red-eye flights across the country or the Atlantic Ocean. One of the better airlines provided sleeping masks. I've saved a few, thinking that one day I could take a nap during the middle of the day while the kids are at school. (For the Moms out there, please don't laugh at my naïveté.)

So what to do with those sleeping masks, you ask? Make a pair of cat ears. Or dog ears, but you can figure that one out on your own.

Materials

1 small piece pink felt (3 × 5 inches)
1 sleeping mask
Fabric glue
1 black T-shirt (adult size)
Black thread
4 pairs hooks and eyes salvaged from an old skirt or blouse
1 skein hairy or fuzzy black yarn
1 pair of black tights or thick stockings (adult size)

Tools

Scissors
Binder clips or clothespins
Sewing needle
Straight pins

Tip

• Purchase a long-sleeved black turtleneck shirt that is one size bigger than what your child normally wears. The sleeves should be slightly long, touching the knuckles. This will allow you to cut thumb notches at the ends of the sleeves, which would give your child's hands the appearance of cat's paws. Paint your child's fingernails white for a more pawlike effect.

The ears

1. Take the **pink felt** and cut out two triangles, each with a base 2 inches wide and a height of 1½ inches.

2. Using the fabric glue, glue the pink triangles on the sleeping mask, each one at opposite

ends and slightly turned inward. Crease the triangles in the middle and be sure to glue them on the mask with a slight pinch. You might need binder clips or clothespins to hold the triangles in place while the glue dries. These are the ears.

The vest

3. Flatten out the **T-shirt** on your worktable so the front is facing up. With a pair of scissors and starting at the bottom edge, cut up the center, being careful to only cut the front of the shirt.

4. Sew up the newly cut edges with the needle and **thread.** This is the opening of the vest. On the edge of the left side, sew the **hooks.** Be sure they are evenly spaced, starting from the top.

5. Have your child try on the vest. Pull the left side over to the right and mark where it fits appropriately. Attach pins to mark where the eyes should be sewn.

6. After your child has taken off the vest, sew the **eyes** onto the right side of the vest. Remove the pins.

7. Cut up the **yarn** into 3-inch pieces. Open the vest so that the back is facing up. Glue the yarn onto the vest. Do it one row at a time, starting at the bottom. Be sure the rows overlap. Set aside and allow for the glue to dry overnight.

The tail

8. Cut off the legs of the **tights.** Set one leg aside and discard the rest.

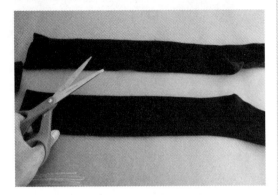

9. Tie a knot at the end of the remaining leg. Starting at the knotted end, glue on the black hairy yarn. Leave at least 4 inches at the opposite end yarn-free. Set aside and allow to dry overnight.

Putting it all together

10. Once all the glue is dry on both the vest and the tail, have your child try on the vest again. While the vest is still undone, take the second leg and tie it around your child's waist. This will be the belt that holds the tail in place. Close the vest.

11. Turn your child so that the back of the vest is facing you. Feel the back for the belt around your child's waist. Mark with a pin where the center of the belt meets the vest. Have your child remove the vest as well as the belt.

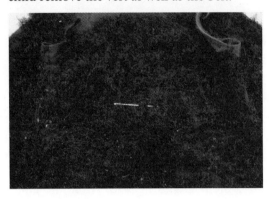

12. Carefully cut a 1-inch slit where the pin is on the back of the vest. Be sure you do not cut the belt. Remove the pin.

13. Push the yarn-free end of the tail through the slit. Attach it to the belt either by sewing it or simply tying it.

14. Have your child try on the ears, vest, and belt with tail attached. Make any adjustments to the costume.

41. Fairy Wings

OKAY, THESE CAN be butterfly wings, too. But having been there (and done that), I know that most little girls want to be a fairy rather than a butterfly. It might have to do with the ability to grant wishes, or having access to your teeth when you leave them under the pillow, or all the sparkles that usually accompany all things in fairyland.

One of the many positives of making your own set of fairy wings is that you can make more than just one. Because all your little girl's playmates will want to be a fairy, too. And it would be a lonely place if only one person got to be the fairy.

Materials

Yellow duct tape (2-inch-wide roll)
4 bamboo skewers, 12 inches long
2 small paper clips
Newspaper
White tempera paint, plus other colors
Glitter
1 empty paper towel roll
1 pair stockings (adult size)
White glue

Tools

Scissors	Pencil
Chain-nose pliers	Craft knife
Round-nose pliers	Awl

Tips

- Add streamers (see page 122) to the ends for an extra fancy touch. It'll make dancing and jumping that much more fun.

The wing frames

1. Align two of the **skewers** on a horizontal plane with the pointed ends facing each other. Using **duct tape,** connect the two skewers in the middle. Repeat on the remaining two skewers.

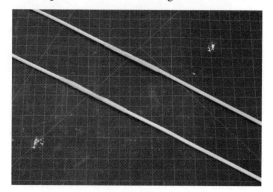

2. Unwind the **paper clips** to make straight lines. Using the chain-nose and round-nose pliers, twist one end of a paper clip to form a closed loop approximately ¼ inch in diameter. The loop should overlap itself. Repeat on the other paper clip.

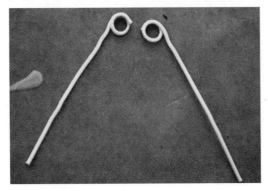

3. Push one of the bamboo skewers through one of the paper clip loops until it reaches the taped middle. Bend at the taped middle so the attached skewer is at a 90-degree angle. Twist the loose end of the paper clip around the bamboo skewer, securing it in place. Repeat on the other pair of bamboo skewers and paper clip. These are the wing frames.

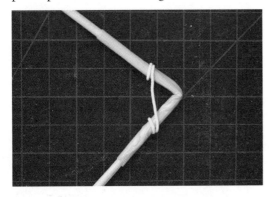

The wings

4. Lay at least eight sheets of unfolded newspaper on your worktable. Place one of the wing frames on top of the newspaper sheets. Keep the bent side off the newspaper so that the paper clip will be left exposed. With a pencil, draw the outline of one fairy wing around the wing frame.

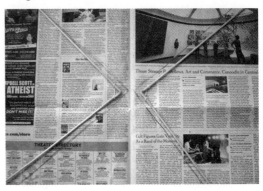

5. Remove the wing frame. With a craft knife, carefully cut the shape of the wing through all eight sheets of newspaper.

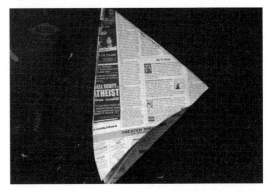

6. Take four of the sheets and flop them from right to left.

7. Place the wing frames in between the newspaper sheets, two sheets on top and two sheets below the frame.

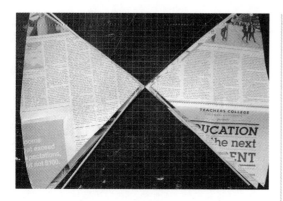

8. Take the points of the frame to the edges of the newspaper sheets. Be sure the bent side with the paper clip remained exposed. These are the unattached wings.

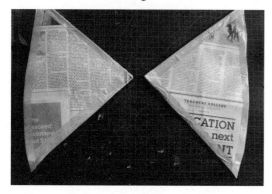

9. Paint the fronts of the wings in **white paint.** Allow the paint to dry, and then paint the other side.

10. Once paint is dry, decorate the front and back of the wings with **other paint colors** and **glitter.**

11. Add duct tape around the border of the wings.

The base

12. Wrap the **empty paper towel roll** in duct tape. With a craft knife, make two slits approximately 1-inch long on opposite sides around the middle of the roll. This is the base.

13. Insert the bent side of the wings with the paper clip into the slits. Tape the slits shut. Make sure the paper clips are not inside the paper towel roll and that there are two openings near the base.

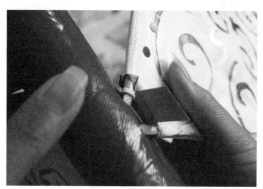

14. Cut off one of the legs of the **stocking.** Loop it through the two openings of the wings near the base and tie back together. These are the armholes.

42. A Family of Ghosts on a String

HERE IS A QUICK and easy Halloween decoration that looks scarier as the day turns into night. You can usually hang these outside your home, but don't worry if it rains. Just hang them by your windows and turn off the lights. If you have night-lights, use them indoors near the windows. And turn on a fan to give your ghosts some movement.

Materials

Newspaper
4 white garbage bags
4 pieces twine or string, approximately 2 feet
  long
1 tie
1 wig
1 skein yarn
Baseball cap or old hat
4 paper clips
1 piece twine, 8 feet long

Tools

Scissors   Awl
Permanent markers   Chain-nose pliers
Safety pins

Tip

- If you don't want to use a tie or don't have any yarn or a wig, use whatever you have around the home to personalize the ghosts. An apron or a football jersey, a ballet tutu, or a hockey mask.

The dad ghost

1. Crumple up a few sheets of **newspaper** until you have a ball around the size of a head. Insert into the bottom of one of the **garbage bags.**

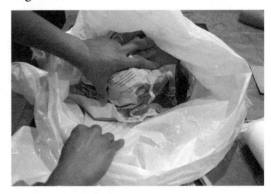

2. Using one piece of the **twine,** tie around the bag and the bottom of the crumpled newspaper. Be sure you are tying the twine around the newspaper and not beneath it or else the twine will fall right off the bag.

3. Using the scissors, cut the bottom of the bag, making jagged edges.

4. Decorate the face with the markers. Add the necktie around the neck. Set aside.

The mom ghost

5. Repeat steps 1 through 3.

6. Secure the **wig** to the head with **safety pins** and decorate the face with the markers. Set aside.

The daughter ghost

7. Repeat steps 1 through 3, but be sure the head is slightly smaller.

8. Decorate the face with the markers. Cut and glue the yarn on the head, long enough to make two braids. Set aside.

The son ghost

9. Repeat steps 1 through 3, but be sure the head is slightly smaller.

10. Decorate the face with the markers. Secure the cap or hat to the head with safety pins.

Putting it all together

11. At the top of the ghosts' heads, poke a hole and push a **paper clip** all the way through until it comes out the other side. Repeat with the other ghosts and clips. Twist the ends of each paper clip so that a small loop forms. Be sure the loop is closed.

12. Take the Dad ghost and attach it to the twine through the paper clip loop. Tie a knot around the paper clip loop and leave a 4-foot tail of twine.

13. Add the rest of the ghosts to the twine, leaving 18 inches between each one. Tie knots around the paper clip loops.

14. After the last ghost has been secured to the twine, hang up your family of ghosts in front of your house.

43. Paper Bat Mobile

I GUESS it's all in the way you say it, but most people think that this is a car craft. I think that I would get royally sued for some sort of copyright infringement if that were true. But this is a mobile (as in the Calder type) of bats.

Materials

Used 8½ × 11-inch printer paper or other
    white paper ready for the recycle bin
Black watercolor paint
1 roll nylon string
2 bamboo skewers, 12 inches long
String, 4 feet
1 screw eye

Tools

Round-nose pliers   Scissors
Chain-nose pliers   Paintbrush

Tip

- If you don't have any watercolors, try using black food coloring or a leaky black ink pen.

The bats

1. Take a piece of **used printer paper** and rip it in half to yield two 5½ × 8½-inch rectangles. Set aside one rectangle.

2. To make a square out of this rectangle, take one side and fold at the corner at a 45-degree angle to meet the perpendicular side. You should have formed a right triangle.

3. There should be excess paper outside of the triangle. Fold and rip off the excess paper. When you open the paper, you should now have a square.

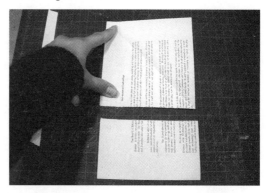

4. Fold square in half. Fold again in half so you form a smaller square.

5. Open the paper so that you are back to one fold. You should have a rectangle again. Position the paper so the folded edge is at the top.

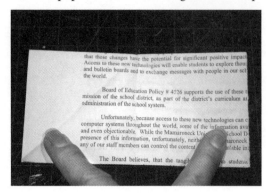

6. Take one side and fold at the top middle crease along the folded edge. When making the fold, do so at a 45-degree angle to meet the perpendicular middle crease line. Repeat on the other side. You should have a triangle.

7. Undo the diagonal folds and fold in the other direction. Then unfold the paper back to the rectangle.

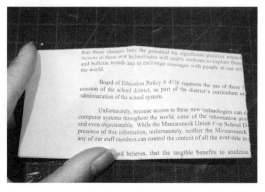

8. Push in both sides of the paper to form the triangle in step 6, but the folds are inverted. (This is called a "mountain fold" in origami-speak.)

9. Take the top triangle "arms" and fold them inward so the outer edges meet in the middle crease. This is the body of the bat and the bottom triangles are the wings.

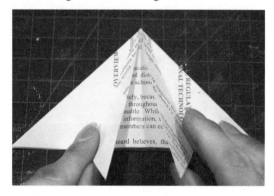

10. Take the top point and fold down about ½ inch. This is the head of the bat. Cut slits

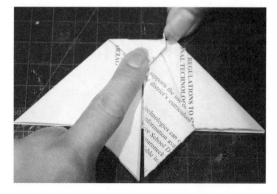

along the top folded edge at the right and left. Pull up the corners. These are the ears of the bat.

11. Repeat steps 1 through 10 until you have twelve bats. Paint the bats with **black watercolor paint.** Allow them to dry.

The mobile

12. Attach **nylon string** to each bat. Each piece of nylon string should be at least 12 inches long.

13. Tie six of the bats to one **bamboo skewer.** Be sure to hang them at different lengths so they will not get tangled up. Set aside.

14. Tie six of the bats to the second bamboo skewer, leaving space in the middle. Then attach the first bamboo skewer to the middle of the second skewer with a nylon string. Hang the mobile with regular string from the ceiling with a screw eye.

November

Projects This Month

Brown Bag Coasters

Thanksgiving Wreath

Fleece Mittens

Crayon Candle

THERE'S A WHOLE LOT OF SHOPPING going on in November. Maybe you've begun your holiday shopping, but it's mostly food that's on your mind. Hmmm, I wonder why. There are brown grocery bags laying around, folded neatly and taking up space because you are now trained to save *everything*. And good for you.

This month, you'll take those brown grocery bags and put them to good use. Oh, sure, you can cook your Thanksgiving turkey in one of the bags, but what about the other dozen or so? Well, I've got a few ideas. And speaking of Thanksgiving, you can certainly use some things that would cozy up the living room.

Materials you will need this month

20 brown flat paper bag handles

1 skein embroidery floss

24 small round nonskid adhesive pads

1 large brown paper grocery bag

At least 12 leaves, in various colors

1 small piece corrugated board

String or yarn

Lots o' broken crayons

1 piece linen thread, approximately 2 inches taller than your jar

1 essential oil, such as lavender

1 tall white candle

1 small glass jar (jelly or artichoke jar)

November holidays, typical and not-so

Daylight Savings (1st Sunday)
National Deviled Egg Day (2nd)
Waiting for the Barbarians Day (4th)
Dunce Day (8th)
Chaos Never Dies Day (9th)
National Pizza with the Works Except Anchovies Day (12th)
National Indian Pudding Day (13th)
National Clean Out Your Refrigerator Day (15th)
Take a Hike Day (17th)
Occult Day (18th)
Have a Bad Day Day (19th)
Absurdity Day (20th)
Start Your Own Country Day (22nd)
Thanksgiving (4th Thursday)
Square Dance Day (29th)
Stay at Home Because You're Well Day (30th)

Monthlong celebrations

Aviation Month
Child Safety and Protection Month
Good Nutrition Month
International Drum Month
Peanut Butter Lover's Month
Latin American Month
National Adoption Month
National Epilepsy Month
National Model Railroad Month
Slaughter Month

November birthdays of famous people

Warren G. Harding (2nd)
James K. Polk (2nd)
Daniel Boone (2nd)
Will Rogers (4th)
Sam Shepard (5th)
Madame Curie (7th)
Kurt Vonnegut, Jr. (11th)
Louis Brandeis (13th)
Claude Monet (14th)
Georgia O'Keeffe (15th)
Martin Scorsese (17th)
James Garfield (19th)
Robert F. Kennedy (20th)
René Magritte (21st)
Franklin Pierce (23rd)
Zachary Taylor (24th)
Joe DiMaggio (25th)
Charles Schulz (26th)
Adam Clayton Powell, Jr. (29th)
Mark Twain (30th)

44. Brown Bag Coasters

LET'S SAY THAT you're hosting Thanksgiving dinner this year and don't have enough coasters for the drinks that all your guests will be absentmindedly leaving around your home. What to do?

You've obviously been grocery shopping, so you probably have lots of brown paper grocery bags. Although you may use the bag part for cooking the turkey or covering up your kitchen counters, the handles are usually an afterthought. Well, think again. These coasters use up all those handles that would otherwise wind up in the recycle bin. So save the precious surfaces of your coffee table, side tables, bookcase, or fireplace mantel.

Materials

20 flat paper brown paper bag handles
1 skein embroidery floss
24 small round nonskid adhesive pads
Colored duct tape, 2 inches wide

Tools

Scissors
Pencil
Ruler

Awl
Thick sewing needle

Tips

- Try coloring the brown bag handles with splashes of watercolor paint before you embroider the words.
- Rub candle wax on the surface to make them water resistant.

The coasters

1. With the scissors, cut the **brown bag handles** into 3¾-inch strips. Discard any extra pieces. You should have sixty strips.

2. Take five of the strips and line them up next to one another, back side facing up.

3. Take five more strips, also back side facing up, and weave them through the first five strips. Place a piece of **duct tape** across the strips as you weave to hold them together. You should have a 3¾-inch square. This is the coaster.

4. Flip over the coaster. Trim any uneven pieces around the edges.

5. With a pencil and ruler, lightly draw a smaller square that is approximately ¼ inch from the outer edge of the coaster.

6. Starting from one corner and using the awl, poke holes along edges of the smaller square.

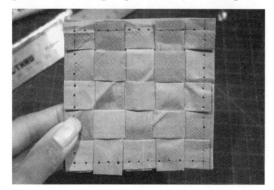

7. Thread a needle with the **embroidery floss.** Push the needle through one of the corner holes, starting from the back side.

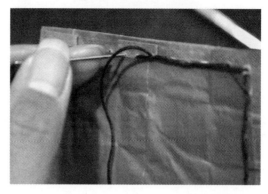

8. Embroider a border along the coaster's edge, putting the needle through the holes.

9. Repeat steps 2 through 8. You should have six coasters.

10. On three coasters, write the word "GIVE" in the center.

11. On the other three coasters, write the word "THANKS" in the center.

12. Poke holes over the words on the coasters, spacing the holes approximately ⅛ inch apart.

13. Starting from the backside, push your threaded needle through one of the holes and embroider the word on the coasters.

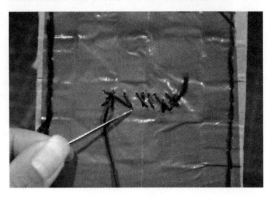

14. Once you are done embroidering, knot the ends. Attach four **nonskidding adhesive pads** to the back of each coaster.

45. Thanksgiving Wreath

You probably have one brown paper grocery bag that you can spare for this wreath. And that's all it takes, one bag to make one wreath. It's pretty amazing to see what you can make out of one grocery bag.

At least 12 leaves, in various colors
1 small piece corrugated board
White acrylic paint
String or yarn
White glue

Materials

1 large brown paper grocery bag
Watercolor paint (choose autumn colors, such as yellow, orange, red, and brown)

Tools

Scissors
Metal ruler, 24-inch
Brushes

Artist's white tape
Awl
Thin paintbrush

Tips

- If you were unable to collect leaves for this project, you can always make them out of brown paper and paint them with watercolors.
- Add petroleum jelly to the leaves to prevent them from drying up too soon.

The wreath

1. Remove the handles from the **bag** and undo the bag at the seams.

2. Flatten the bag across your work space and cut lengthwise into eight 2-inch strips.

3. Take one strip and fold in half lengthwise. Fold again. Then tightly twist it to form a rope.

4. Use **white glue** to glue the ends together to form a circle. Allow time for the glue to dry.

5. Paint the rope with a single color of watercolor paint. Allow time for the paint to dry.

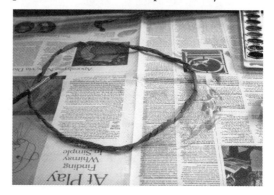

6. Take each of the remaining 2-inch strips and tightly twist them into ropes.

7. Tape the ropes to a clean surface. Be sure you have newspaper or other waste paper covering your work area and that the ropes are twisted tightly.

8. Paint the ropes with watercolors, choosing single colors for each one. Allow time for the paint to dry.

9. Remove one rope and weave it around the circle made by the first rope in step 4. Glue the ends together.

10. Repeat step 9 until all the ropes are woven together. This is the wreath.

11. Glue the **leaves** to the wreath.

12. Cut down the **corrugated board** to 4½ × 2 inches. Paint with watercolors and allow time for it to dry.

13. With white acrylic paint and a thin paintbrush, write "Happy Thanksgiving" across the board.

14. Poke holes on the sides of the board and thread with the string. Attach the board to the wreath and hang on the front of your door.

46. Fleece Mittens

MITTENS ARE ESSENTIAL accessories during the colder months of the year. Wouldn't it be great to stock your own supply of mittens? At least once in your life, you will misplace a glove or mitten. It usually happens at an inopportune moment, like when you are running late and need to catch a train to work. And fervently cursing under your breath will not make your naked hand any warmer.

Have you wondered what to do with all those fleece pullovers or pants that your children have outgrown or fallen out of fashion? This is the perfect project for you.

Materials

Brown paper grocery bag
Fleece fabrics, from an old vest, blanket, pants, or pullover, large enough to make eight 9-inch squares
1 skein of embroidery floss, any color

Tools

Pencil
Scissors
Thick sewing needle

Tips

• The fabric measurements are for an average-size ladies' pair of mittens. For children, use 7 inch squares of fabric. For men's, use 10 inch squares.

• Try stitching a loop at the base of the mittens so you can hang them up.

The mittens

1. Place your hand on top of the brown paper grocery bag and trace the outline with a pencil.

2. Cut away the excess paper. This is your mitten pattern.

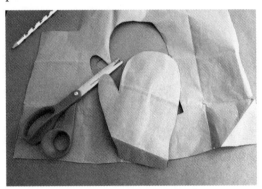

3. Cut out eight 9-inch squares from the fleece fabrics.

4. Using the pattern, cut out eight mitten pieces out of the eight fleece squares.

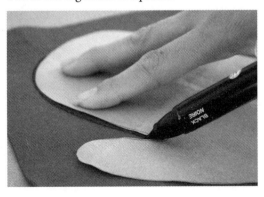

5. Sew two of the mitten pieces together. Be sure that the base of the mitten piece is left open.

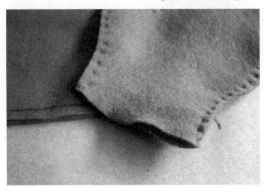

6. Repeat step 5 until you have four sewn mitten shells.

7. Place one mitten shell on top of another, lining up the thumbs and outer edges. Make a few stitches at the top borders of the mittens, connecting them.

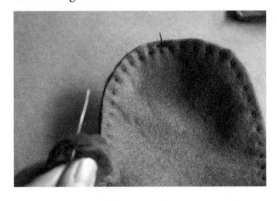

8. Choose which one of the two sewn mitten shells will be the outer one. Turn it inside out

10. Sew the inner and outer shells of both mittens together at the base.

so that the inner shell is covered by the outer shell. The stitches should not be exposed.

9. Repeat steps 7 and 8 on the remaining two mitten shells.

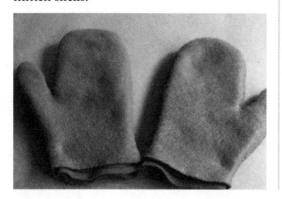

47. Crayon Candle

SOMEWHERE IN THE HOUSE, in the car, in your kids' closets, in the backyard, and even in your purse, there's a broken crayon. And everywhere you go, there are crayons for the taking, at school, at a party, at a kid-friendly restaurant, in the dressing room of a department store that caters to multitasking Moms, or even at the gym that provides babysitting while you run your heart out on the treadmill. Crayons, crayons, crayons.

Instead of throwing them out, I save them—because I know what beautiful candles they make. So get out a jar and place it on your kitchen windowsill. Every time you pull a crayon out of thin air (which is more often than you want to believe), put it in the jar. Pretty soon you'll be making these crayon candles for friends and family alike.

Materials

1 piece linen thread, approximately 2 inches taller than your jar

1 essential oil, such as lavender

1 tall white candle

Lots o' broken crayons

1 small glass jar (jelly or artichoke jar)

Tools

Paper towel
A 1-gallon sealable
  plastic bag
Hammer

Cellophane
Matches or a lighter
Scissors

Tip

- If you are an experienced candle maker, you can make these candles faster by using boiling bags and white paraffin (wax).

The wick

1. Soak the **thread** in the **essential oil.** Rub off any excess oil with a paper towel. Let the thread sit on the paper towel for 20 minutes or so.

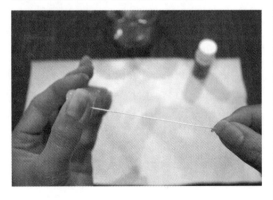

2. Thoroughly wax the thread by running it across the bottom of the **white candle** a few times. This is the wick. Set it aside.

3. Select the **crayon** colors that you want and remove all paper. Place the crayons in the 1-gallon sealable plastic bag.

4. With a hammer, gently break the crayons into little pieces, almost until you get pieces that are like sand.

Filling the jar

5. Fill the **jar** one-quarter of the way with broken crayon pieces and add the wick to the center.

6. With a piece of cellophane, press down on the crayon pieces, compressing them so there is less space.

7. Light the white candle and allow time for some liquid wax to build at the top.

8. When there is approximately 1 tablespoon of hot wax at the top of the candle, pour it into the jar. Once you have poured all the wax, return the candle to the upright position so that more hot wax can build up. Repeat until you have covered the broken crayon pieces.

9. Add another layer of more broken crayon pieces to the jar, until it's about halfway filled. Again, be sure that the wick is centered in the jar.

10. Repeat steps 6 through 8.

11. Keep adding layers of broken crayon pieces and repeating steps 6 through 8 until the jar is filled.

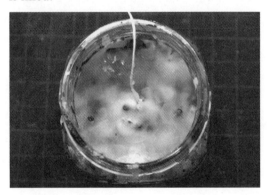

12. Trim the wick down to ½-inch.

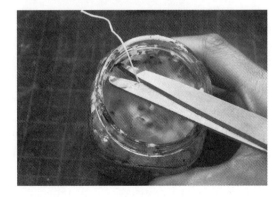

December

Projects This Month

Photo Album

'Tis the Season Holiday Card

Photo Ornament Ball

Holiday Cracker

Button-n-Paper Bead Bracelet

THIS IS THE MONTH that we've all been waiting for. Oh, yes, we've been crafting all year, but when December arrives it's like we've been on a pilgrimage and reached our destination. The Holidays (with a capital H): Hanukkah, Christmas, Kwanzaa, or Festivus. (I'm sure that I'm missing one or two, so please forgive the oversight.) It's the time we make holiday cards, gifts for our family and friends, and home decorations with such fervent passion that it seems we are possessed.

Many crafts in this book would make great little gifts: a notepad, a little wallet, a necklace, a handbag, or a picture frame. And there are decorations that you can slightly adjust to make them more appropriate for the holidays, too, such as the paper lantern (give it a more snowflake look) or the Thanksgiving wreath (a simple change of color scheme). Here are a few more great crafts to add to the list, and boy, what a list you have by now.

Materials you will need this month

2 sheets acid-free watercolor paper (22 × 30 inches)

2 large cereal boxes

1 large paper gift bag (plain color)

Linen thread

Embroidery floss

Double-sided Mylar (you will need to buy this)

Lots o' white cardboard (from food boxes—can be printed on one side and white on the other)

Picture of a snowflake (from a magazine or the Web)

8 photos

8 beads (with hole large enough for the floss)

6 empty toilet paper rolls

1 roll gift wrap

12 pieces of ribbon, 6 inches long

6 sheets tissue paper

1 bag individually wrapped candy

December holidays, typical and not-so

Wear Brown Shoes Day (4th)

National Gazpacho Day (6th)

Pearl Harbor Day (7th)

National Pastry Day (9th)

National Ding-a-Ling Day (12th)

Ice Cream and Violins Day (11th)

National Chocolate-Covered Anything Day (16th)

Underdog Day (17th)

Hanukkah (varies every year; check a calendar or the Web)

National Roast Suckling Pig Day (18th)

Games Day (20th)

National Flashlight Day (21st)

Festivus (23rd)

National Egg Nog Day and Christmas Eve (24th)

Christmas (25th)

National Whiners Day (26th)

Kwanzaa (December 26–January 1)

National Fruitcake Day (27th)

National Chocolate Day (28th)

Festival of Enormous Changes at the Last Minute (30th)

New Year's Eve (31st)

Monthlong celebrations

Hi Neighbor Month

National Stress-Free Family Holiday Month

Bingo's Birthday Month

Read a New Book Month

December birthdays of famous people

Charles Ringling (2nd)	Frank Zappa (21st)
Georges Seurat (2nd)	Howard Hughes (24th)
Walt Disney (5th)	Cab Calloway (25th)
Martin Van Buren (5th)	Humphrey Bogart (25th)
Ira Gershwin (6th)	Robert Ripley (25th)
Sammy Davis, Jr. (8th)	Clara Barton (25th)
Emily Dickinson (10th)	Sir Isaac Newton (25th)
Margaret Mead (16th)	Louis Pasteur (27th)
Noel Coward (16th)	Woodrow Wilson (28th)
Jane Austen (16th)	Andrew Johnson (29th)
Ludwig van Beethoven (16th)	Rudyard Kipling (30th)
Steven Spielberg (18th)	Henri Matisse (31st)

48. Photo Album

THESE MAKE GREAT GIFTS for Grandma. This project requires that you head to an art supply store to purchase a sheet of watercolor paper. The kind that I like to use is made by Arches. It's a 140-pound cold-press sheet made of 100% cotton. You can select a natural white or a bright white. There's a blind emboss of the company logo at the bottom corner of the sheet, and the sheets have these rough unfinished edges. I like to incorporate both elements into the design of the album, but you can certainly trim them off if you want to. It's important to buy acid-free paper for any photo album that you make, because any acid content in the paper will slowly destroy your photos.

Materials

- 2 sheets acid-free watercolor paper (22 × 30 inches)
- 2 large cereal boxes
- "The mix" (see page xvi)
- 1 large paper gift bag (plain color)
- Linen thread
- Embroidery floss

Tools

Paper cutter	1-inch paintbrush
Metal ruler, 24 inches long	Awl
	Thick sewing needle
Craft knife	Pencil
Bone folder	Waxed paper

Tip

- You can buy the photo corners or simply cut small slits into the pages to hold the photos. If you do cut small slits, be sure to accommodate the photos on the other side of the sheet.

The book pages/signatures

1. With the paper cutter, quarter one of the **watercolor paper sheets** to make four 15 × 11-inch pieces. Cut the other one in half to be 30

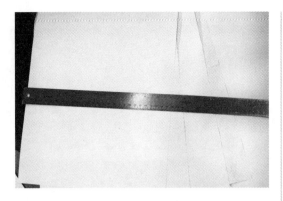

× 11 inches. Set one half aside for the end sheet (see step 13 below). Take the remaining half and cut in half to make two 15 × 11-inch pieces. You should have six pieces altogether.

2. Fold each piece further to be 7½ × 11 inches. Reinforce each crease with the bone folder to get a tight fold. These are the book pages. There should be 12 sheets or 24 pages (front and back of the sheet). Group them into three sets, each with two sheets or four pages. These are your signatures. Set them aside.

3. Undo the cereal boxes at the seams and flatten them out. Set one box aside. Apply a thin layer of "the mix" on one side of the remaining box. Add the second box on top and smooth out any air pockets with the bone folder. Allow enough time for the adhesive to dry.

The book boards

4. Cut down the box into two 8 × 11½-inch rectangles and one ½ × 11½-inch rectangle. These are the book boards.

Making the case

Please note steps 7 through 9 should be done quickly to avoid premature drying of the adhesive; read through the instructions before proceeding.

5. Undo the gift bag at the seams and lay flat, back side facing up. Lay the metal ruler across the bottom.

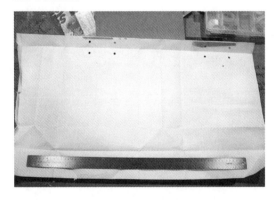

6. Take one 8 × 11½-inch board and apply a thin layer of "the mix" to one side. With the glue side facing down, place the board on top of the gift bag. The bottom edge should be 8 inches long and should sit flush against the top edge of the metal ruler.

7. Take the ½ × 11½-inch rectangle and apply a thin layer of "the mix" to one side. With the glue side facing down, place the board on top of the gift bag, the ½-inch side sitting flush against the top edge of the ruler, ¹⁄₁₆ inch to the right of the first board.

8. Take the last 8 × 11½-inch board and apply a thin layer of "the mix" to one side. With the glue side facing down, place the board on top of the gift bag, the 8-inch side sitting flush against the top edge of the ruler, ¹⁄₁₆ inch to the right of the second board.

9. Quickly flip over the gift bag paper and smooth out any air pockets with the bone folder.

10. Flip over again so the boards are facing up. Using the metal ruler as a guide, remove any excess bag paper around the boards, leaving a margin that is as wide as the ruler. This is the case.

11. About ⅛ inch from the points of each board, cut off the four corners of margin around the case at a 45-degree angle. Apply a thin layer of "the mix" to the margin around the case and pull it tightly over the boards. Smooth out any air pockets with the bone folder.

The book block

12. Cut a piece of scrap paper about 2 inches wide and 11 inches tall. Fold in half lengthwise to be 1 × 11 inches. Along the crease, punch five equidistant holes with the awl. Mark the top

and the bottom. This is the sewing pattern. Nest the sewing pattern inside each signature and punch holes into the crease.

13. Take the remaining half sheet of watercolor paper and place it lengthwise on your worktable. The 30-inch side should be at the bottom. Starting on the left side, measure and mark 7½ inches on the top and bottom edges. Connect the two points vertically with the metal ruler, then score and fold the sheet. From the 7½-inch mark, measure ½ inch at the top and bottom of the sheet. Connect the two points vertically with the metal ruler, then score and fold the sheet. Then measure 7½ inches from this fold and mark it on the top and bottom edge. Connect the two points vertically with the metal ruler and cut off the excess paper to the right with a craft knife.

14. Inside the middle ½-inch-wide space, you will be sewing the signatures. Draw three equidistant lines vertically within this space. Using

your sewing pattern as a guide, poke five holes on each line. Sew each signature to one line using a pamphlet stitch (see page 5). Be sure to start from the backside. This is the book block.

Putting it all together

15. Take this time to design something on the front panel of the case. It can be the word "Grandma" or "Happy Holidays." Poke holes with the awl and embroider it.

16. Once you are done with your design, apply a thin layer of "the mix" to the back side of the book block. Nest it inside the case and smooth out any air pockets with the bone folder. Be sure to get the spaces in between the signatures. Place a piece of waxed paper between the sheets until the adhesive is dry.

49. 'Tis the Season Holiday Card

MAKING CARDS for fifty people is not an easy task, but as a crafter, you feel indebted to give it the old college try. Or if you've done it before, there's the added pressure of trying to either adequately repeat or even top yourself.

I've decided early on that the best way to create holiday cards en masse is to make a stencil. It's easy: you pour all your creative juices into one thing that helps you replicate your design over and over again. The trick is to get a good stencil material and not get too fancy. I prefer to use double-sided Mylar, which can be found at any craft or art supply store.

Materials

1 sheet double-sided Mylar
Lots o' white cardboard (from food boxes—can be printed on one side and white on the other)
Picture of a snowflake (from a magazine or the Web)
White and blue acrylic paint

Tools

Pencil
Craft knife
Sponge

Tips

- Have a water bottle and extra clean sponges/cloths handy. Mistakes happen, but can be fixed!
- Tracing images that will be made into a stencil requires that you carve small pieces to mimic a larger surface area. Be sure to keep this in mind when looking for your snowflake picture.

Base cards

1. Cut down cardboard into 5½ × 8½-inch rectangles.
2. Fold rectangles to make 5½ × 4¼-inch cards. The front and back panels are the printed side. The inside panels are the white side.

The stencil

3. Place the Mylar on top of the snowflake picture. Trace the snowflake.

4. With a craft knife, cut out the snowflake.

Prepping base cards

5. With the sponge, apply one coat of white paint onto the front panel of your cards. Allow time for the paint to dry to the touch.

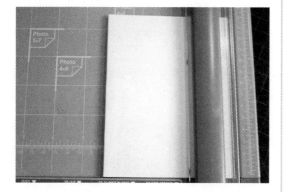

6. With the sponge, apply one coat of blue paint onto the front panel of your cards. Again, allow time for the paint to dry to the touch.

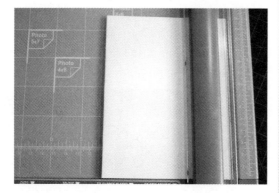

Painting the snowflakes

7. Take one of the cards and place the stencil in the center of the front panel. With a sponge, apply white paint over the stencil so the snowflake appears. Be sure to avoid oversaturating the stencil with paint.

8. Sponge on white snowflakes on other parts of the front panel, spacing them as you like.

9. Repeat steps 5 and 6 on the other cards. Allow time for the paint to dry to the touch.

50. Photo Ball Ornament

EVER WONDER what to do with all those photos your friends and family send during the holidays? Make this ball ornament to hang on your tree or fireplace mantle.

Materials

8 photos
White glue
8 beads (with hole large enough for the floss)
Embroidery floss or yarn

Tools

Vitamin bottle cap   Scissors
Pen   Awl

Tip

- To give this ball ornament a little bit more flair, try using a pair of decorative paper edgers instead of plain scissors.

The photo ball

1. With the bottle cap and pen, circle the area in each **photo** that you want included in the ball ornament.

2. Cut out each circle with a pair of scissors.

3. For each circle, you will be folding in the sides to create an inner triangle. Perfect one and use it as a measurement guide for the other seven circles.

4. Once you are done folding inner triangles in all eight circles, use the **white glue** to attach two circles and one set of flaps together. Be sure that the photos are right side up.

5. Repeat step 4. Create a "cap" with the two glued sets of circles. Again, be sure that all the photos are right side up as much as possible.

6. Repeat steps 4 and 5. You should have two "caps."

7. Glue the two caps together to form a ball. Allow enough time for the glue to dry before proceeding to the next step.

8. With the awl, poke a hole at the bottom of the ball.

9. Thread the needle with an 8-inch piece of embroidery floss. Push the needle completely through the hole. Remove the needle from the

floss and tug at the ends of the floss so each side is even. Tie the ends of the floss into a knot close to the bottom of the ball.

10. Through both ends of the floss, push a bead through until it is 2 inches away from the bottom of the ball. Tie a knot to prevent the bead from falling off.

11. With an awl, poke a hole at the top of the ball.

12. Thread the needle with an 8-inch piece of embroidery floss. Push the needle completely

through the hole. Remove the needle from the floss and tug at the ends of the floss so each side is even. Tie the ends of the floss into a knot close to the top of the ball.

13. Tie another knot in the floss to make a loop.

14. Hang the ball ornament from your tree or mantle to see if you need to make any adjustments.

51. Holiday Crackers

Aside from the little sliver of gunpowder that accounts for the actual cracking sound, these holiday crackers are just like the ones of yore, depending on what your version of yore is. They also make great place cards for a dinner party.

Materials

    6 sheets tissue paper
    Craft glue stick
    1 roll gift wrap
    6 empty toilet paper rolls
    1 bag individually wrapped candy
    12 pieces 6-inch-long ribbon

Tools

    Scissors

Tip

- I sometimes save the little trinkets my kids bring home from birthday parties so that I can fill up these holiday crackers. Although this takes some foresight and patience (and a good memory—

where did I put those whistles?), it pays off when your guests open these holiday crackers and see the silly toys you filled it with.

The crown

1. Take all six sheets of **tissue paper** and fold them in half. Cut out a crown. You should have twelve cut pieces of tissue paper.

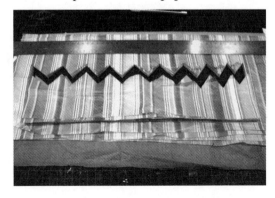

2. Pull off two cut crowns, being careful not to separate them from each other. Glue the ends together. Allow time for the glue to dry.

3. Repeat step 2 until you have six glued crowns.

The main body

4. Cut six rectangles of **gift wrap** measuring 8 × 6 inches. Set aside.

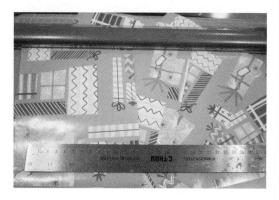

5. Take one toilet paper roll and make an incision lengthwise, then cut it in half down the middle.

6. Take one gift wrap rectangle and place it landscape (8-inch side at the bottom) on your

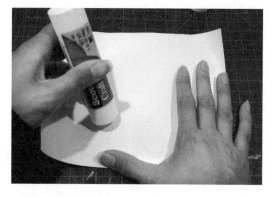

worktable with the printed side down. Apply a thin layer of glue.

7. Place the cut-up toilet paper roll on top. Be sure that it does not overlap in the middle.

8. Pull the bottom edge over the top so that it forms a roll again. Make the roll tighter and smaller than it was previously, to about 1¼ inch diameter.

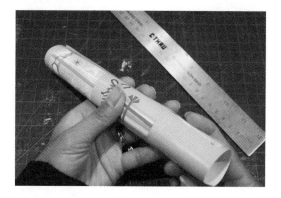

9. Glue the bottom edge in place. This is the main body of the cracker.

Putting it all together

10. Take one of the crowns and fold it down so it can fit inside the cracker. Place it inside.

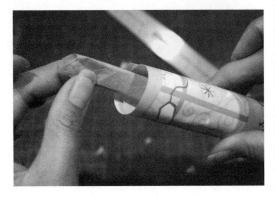

11. Fill the rest of the cracker with candy and other trinkets you may have around the house.

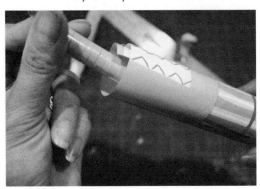

12. Tie the open ends with ribbon.

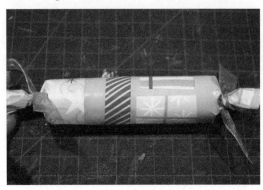

13. Repeat steps 5 through 12 until you have six complete holiday crackers.

14. Personalize each cracker.

52. Button-n-Paper Bead Bracelet

MY NIECE Katie is an avid jewelry maker. She specializes in earrings and necklaces made with beads and wire. I never had the pleasure of bending and twisting wire until Katie showed me the way. Thanks to her, this bracelet exists.

While the proper wire—30 gauge non-tarnish artistic wire—is not a material that you can easily find in your trash, you can make lots of interesting jewelry *with* your trash using wire as the conduit. Beads made from various paper products are probably the most immediate ones.

Materials

1 magazine sheet
White glue
30 gauge non-tarnish artistic wire, 1 spool
3 medium sized round buttons with four holes, at least ¾ inch in diameter

Tools

Pencil	Wire cutters
Ruler	White artists tape
Paper cutter	Chain-nose pliers
2 bamboo skewers	

Tip

- If you want a tighter fitting bracelet, use a salvaged clasp from a broken necklace or bracelet, decrease the amount of paper beads from 54 to 45, and eliminate one of the buttons.

The bracelet

1. Using a ruler and pencil mark ¼-inch increments at the top of one magazine sheet. At the bottom of the sheet, mark ⅛ inch from the right edge, then mark ¼-inch increments thereafter.

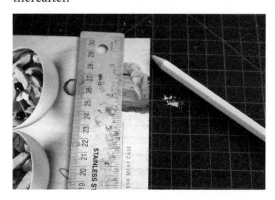

2. Using a paper cutter, cut sheet into long triangles. Use the marks at the top and bottom of the sheet as guides. Cut out 54 triangles plus 5 or 6 extra for mistakes.

3. Add a very thin stream of glue on the back of one triangle. Be sure to leave ¾ inch at the wide end of the triangle glue-free.

4. Starting at the wide end of the triangle, roll the triangle around the bamboo skewer. This is the paper bead.

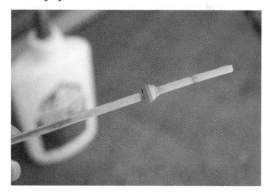

5. Repeat steps 9 and 10 until you have 54 paper beads. You will need the second bamboo skewer to fit all the beads. Brush a thin layer of varnish on the beads and let them dry for at least 3 hours.

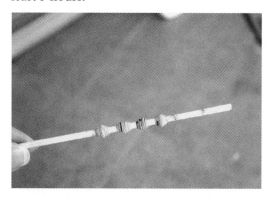

6. Using the wire cutters, cut two strips of artistic wire, each measuring 36 inches.

7. Bend each wire in half. Twist a small loop approximately ⅛ inch in diameter at the bent end of each wire. Tape down the looped ends to your work space.

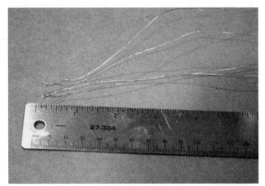

8. There should be four legs of wire. Twist the two inner wires together so that there are now three legs. Insert one bead into each leg.

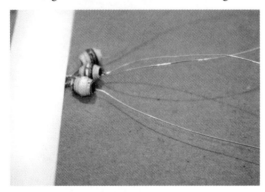

9. Secure the beads in their row by pulling at the two inner legs, tightening the twist that is now

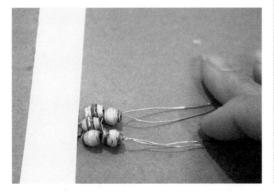

inside the middle bead. Gently pull the two inner legs apart to get four legs again. Then twist the first two wires together and the last two wires together. There are now two legs. Insert one bead into each leg.

10. Secure the beads by pulling at the pair of twisted legs, tightening the twists that are now inside each bead. Gently pull the legs apart to get four legs again.

11. Repeat steps 8 through 10 until you have seven rows of beads in this pattern: 3-2-3-2-3-2-3.

12. Weave a button into the wire.

13. Repeat steps 8 through 10 until you have another section of beads with seven rows in this pattern: 3-2-3-2-3-2-3. Weave a second button into the bracelet by pushing the wire legs through the holes.

14. Repeat steps 8 through 10 until you have a third section of beads with seven rows in this pattern: 3-2-3-2-3-2-3. Weave a third button into the wire into the bracelet by pushing the wire legs through the holes.

15. Twist the first two wires together and the last two wires together. You should have two legs. Push each leg into one of the loops at the beginning of the bracelet. Bend the wire legs around the loops and twist them. Take the ends of the legs and push them inside the beads of the first row in the first section.

Acknowledgments

THERE IS A LONG LIST of people who had a hand in making this book, some more obvious than others.

Thanks to my husband, Dave, the self-proclaimed editor of all things me, whether it's my books or my cooking or even my clothes. Thanks for putting up with the "mess," both literal and metaphorical. Thanks to my son, Mack, a mostly patient boy. His steadfast company was much appreciated as I slugged through the writing of this book. Thanks for letting mommy work. Thanks to my daughter, Masana, herself a genius in all things crafty. I love making stuff with you.

To my mother and father, Norma and Pat Fabian. Thanks for never saying that I couldn't do it, whatever "it" may have been. To my sister, Chonaliza Illonardo. Thanks for all your sage advice and supporting me in everything I do, even if it's yet another crazy "Lucy" scheme. You have been an especially good "Ethel." Thanks to my brothers-in-law, Victor Waka (MacGyver) and Victor Illonardo (Mr. Baseball). Polar Bears rule! Thank you, Katie Waka, my stylish niece. Your jewelry rocks! To my new nieces, Ronica and Haley. Although you may not know it yet, one day you will appreciate my crafty ways. So this is a "thank-you" for the future. To my nephew, Michael Waka, who lent not only his hands but his eyes to this project. Your assistance in photographing the crafts as well as research were much appreciated. Thank you, thank you, thank you, Mike!

A HUGE thanks to my sister, Elleanore Waka, who heralded my work to the "powers-that-be" at Citadel. You have always been my cheerleader and words fail to describe how much you mean to me.

To Charise, my talented and smart friend. Thanks for all your words of encouragement throughout this project. You are my idol. To my young and talented crafters, Amanda, Shea, Zoe, and Noelle, and their moms, Jacqueline, Karen, Julie, and Ginny. Without our little crafting sessions I wouldn't have the crafts in this book! "Sock" monkeys rule. Thank you.

To my agent, Susan Ginsburg: thanks for believing in me. To Amy Pyle, the person who kept me on track when things got rough. Thank you, Amy.

Most of all, I must thank Danielle Chiotti, my editor. Your firm yet gentle guidance on this book made me believe that I am better than I truly am. (How did you do that?) I would do anything for you!

While making the crafts and writing this book, I constantly listened to the music of Duran Duran, Aimee Mann, Annie Lennox, Elvis Costello, The Killers, Muse, Weezer, and Dire Straits. My ears—and hands—would have been sad without you. And who wants to see sad crafts?